Ragged-Edge Flowers

Fast-Folded Ways to Make Textured Quilts

LAURA FARSON

©2002 Laura Farson

Published by

Krause Publications
700 E. State St., Iola,
WI 54990-0001
Telephone 715-445-2214
www.krause.com

Please call or write for our free catalog of publications. Our toll-free number to place an order or obtain a free catalog is 800-258-0929, or please use our regular business telephone 715-445-2214.

Photography by Greg Daniels, unless otherwise noted.
Portrait by Ron Ackerman.
Cover photo by Krause Publications.
Illustrations by Laura Farson.
Line drawing by Susan Corey.
"Crinkly Crib Blanket," constructed by Melania Thompson, 2002.
Projects and Quilts designed and constructed by Laura Farson, 2002.
Editorial Reading by Lynne Beykirch.

Some product names used in this book are registered trademarks: Fray Check™, Thermore®, Olfa®.

Library of Congress Catalog Number: 2002107603

ISBN: 0-87349-500-4

Preface

After seeing the beautiful raggedy quilts that are currently so popular, I couldn't help myself. I had to figure out how to make ragged-edge flowers! It was a perfect excuse to make more quilts.

What surprised me was the diversity of effects that can be made with such a simple construction technique. It started with the "Raggedy Edges Basic Square" from my first book, *Fast-Folded Flowers: Timesaving Techniques for a Quilted Bouquet*. I had cut lots of red plaid squares but ran out of time to complete a quilt. On a lark, I finished it and set about discovering what other flower shapes could be "translated" into ragged edges. Guess what—they all can! With minor adjustments to manage the shredding issue, I've created more flowers and more shapes for you. It's so liberating to leave the center area of the flowers free and fuzzy just like in nature.

I decided that in order for these to be fun, even the joining had to be simple. So I experimented with patches, which were glue basted on the front and back with a little batting. I sewed them into the empty spaces and *voila*, success! After getting all the pieces together with raw edges, I left the binding ragged too.

It's been lots of fun and surprising to see what special effects occur when mixing and matching the fabrics. I've learned not to expect a certain result, because color can play tricks. When I completed the blue and green starry square with the alternating fabric, I expected to see a cross pattern, and lo and behold, I got circles! Surprise!

As promised, I've added two new shapes: rectangles and diamonds. They add even more dimension and optical illusions to the projects. Shape combinations enhance the design possibilities, and the depth created by color and shape adds a bit of whimsy.

Like its predecessor, *Fast-Folded Flowers*, *Ragged-Edge Flowers* gives you plenty of ideas for quilting projects. I encourage you to experiment. Make some flowers, toss them in the laundry, and see what pops up! Have fun!

Dedication

To Russ, for your continued understanding

Acknowledgments

Pfaff American Sales, Kim Fillmore and Pam Shefferman
American and Efird, Marci Brier
Marcus Brothers, Lisa Shepard
AE Nathan, Joel Preefer
Olfa
Prym Dritz
Westfalenstoffe, Sarah Shimota Klein
Timesaver Templates, John Bowling
Hobbs, H. D. Wilbanks
Dream World Sew Steady, The Lindsays
Roxanne

Julie Stephani
Amy Tincher-Durik
Brenda Mazemke
Jodi Rintelman
Marilyn Hochstatter
Pat Steik
Kathy Jennings
Lois Weissberg
Bonnie Jameson
Linda and Tim Lonergan
Leland, the cat

Table of Contents

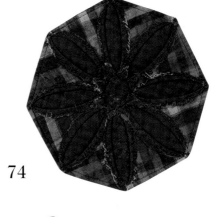

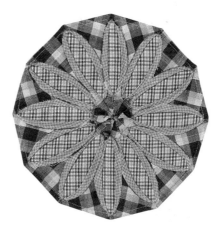

Introduction

Ragged-edge flowers are fast, fun, and easy! There are many choices for shape, technique, fabric, and color. Designs range from simple to complex, but the construction stays easy!

Projects have a myriad of flower shapes formed by folded bias edges of fabric. These unfinished bias edges easily bend to form the curves of the petal edges. When laundered, they bloom into fuzzy, lettuce edges.

Shapes are all cut with bias edges, primarily for ease in turning the petals, and secondarily to control the shredding of the raw edges. Bias causes a fairly-even fraying, where straight grain cutting allows for threads to shred and degrade the integrity of the fabric and the seam line.

All shapes are made using the same basic construction technique. Two fabrics are cut into a defined shape. These fabric pieces are placed right sides out with their edges matching. Corners and/or points are folded and pressed to the center of the shape. The folded edges are then topstitched into dimensional flower petals. These units are joined with "patches" cut to overlap the area between the flowers. All the stitching is done on the sewing machine, and when you finish topstitching the petals, you're done! All the layers are combined during the construction, so there's no cumbersome layering of batting and backing fabric.

Chapter One walks you through the process, step-by-step. Photos and illustrations clarify how to proceed.

Chapters Two through Eight contain instructions on different shapes, ranging from three-sided triangle variations through multi-sided shapes that are versatile, yet simple to make. The four-sided shapes—squares, rectangles, and diamonds—have lots of optical illusions. Since the shapes fit together without joining patches, they cover the whole field with flower petals. Hexagons, Octagons, and the supreme flower petal producer, the dodecagon, make a bounty of colorful flowers.

The emphasis is on simplicity, but the results look complicated. Twelve variations are explained, and each one transforms the fabric into a unique flower unit that's joined with others to complete a bouquet.

The sequence begins with fabric selection and preparation, template construction, batting insertion, folding, petal turning, and topstitching. Three alternative joining options are explained and illustrated.

The simplest designs, squares, are cut with standard-size rotary rulers. The remaining shapes are cut with templates. These templates are made from photocopies of the full-size patterns in the appendix. The patterns are cut from the paper and, when necessary, parts are taped together. The templates have been designed to maximize the use of fabric, so they are sized to fit between the fold and selvedge of 45" or 60" wide fabric. Cut offs are recycled into patches.

The paper template is placed on the fabric, rotated to create bias edges. Temporary adhesive spray is used to secure the templates on the fabric while the pieces are being cut.

Batting is included in projects made from thinner homespun or shirting fabrics. Batting pieces are cut to fit inside the center area of each unit and incorporated in the unit construction, rather than being layered between a pieced top and backing fabric. This makes maneuvering much simpler. A light thin batting like Hobbs Thermore works best with the brushed, woven, and homespun fabrics used in these projects.

Corners or points are folded into flowery geometric shapes and secured with topstitching. Many stitch choices can be used to form the petals. The degree of fray is determined by the

placement of the stitching. Straight stitching leaves lots of fabric to fluff, while zigzag or overcast hemstitching limits the exposed raw edges and makes a scalloped effect.

Joining can be invisible when the units are sewn together in the folds before the top-stitching steps. This method is a bit more cumbersome but has the advantage of being a softer seam. Some shapes are more easily joined with simple zigzag topstitching across the common areas of the sides. These shapes are filled in with layered patches. Patches are attached to the back of the project, overlapping the gaps. On the front side, a batting cutout is layered in the gap and a front patch is placed on top of it. All the layers are sewn through with a zigzag or hemstitch. The overcastting stitches secure all the layers of the patch to the main body of the project.

As an alternative to the zigzag topstitching, units can be joined with an edge overcast zigzag. The units to be joined are placed one on top of the other with the seam edges aligned. The zigzag stitches are placed so that the right swing of the needle is off the edge of the fabric. The left swing pierces both units. When the units are opened flat, the stitching on the front side looks like a tiny ladder. The stitches practically disappear when using matching thread. These seams are strong, yet flexible.

A single layer of bias-cut binding is sewn to the outer edges. The edge facing the front is left raw to frame the projects with ragged edges.

Finished projects are washed and dried to "bloom" the ragged edges, creating the three-dimensional texture.

After the basic technique, instructions move on to enhanced versions: A third fabric can be added to any shape to create outlines around the petals. The fabric cutout that's layered under the folded flaps can be made with more exotic fabrics, like chenille, terrycloth, fake fur, or ultra suede. Overlays of lace and curtain fabrics also make lovely effects.

Each chapter features at least one project for each technique. There are variations in size and color and fabric choice. Read through the instructions and make up some sample blocks. Vary the fabric choices and stitch styles. Launder them to get the full effect.

Make four of your favorites into a pillow. Move up to a baby blanket or throw. Once you start, you'll want to make more and more. Happily, they make great gifts.

Do have fun and enjoy the results!

1 How to Make *Ragged-Edge Flowers*

Whatever your favorite shape or design, all of the ragged-edge flowers can be completed after mastering only a few simple techniques. Each flower is composed of two fabrics that are cut with a template or ruler. With wrong sides together and the edges matching, the corners and/or points are folded and pressed to the center of the shape. The folded edges are then topstitched into dimensional flower petals. These units are either joined to each other or joined with "patches" cut to fit between the flowers. The term "unit" refers to the layered, folded, and sometimes top-stitched-packet of fabric and batting (when included).

Tools and Supplies

These basic tools and supplies are essential for making ragged-edge flowers:
- Iron
- Silk pins
- Rotary cutter, 45mm
- Rotary point cutter
- Rotary rulers (1" x 12", 12½" square, 6" x 24" rectangle)
- Rotary cutting mat (18" x 24")
- Paper and pencils
- Sewing machine
- Walking foot or dual feed feature on sewing machine
- Sewing machine needles—quilting 90/14, metallic, and embroidery for decorative threads
- Bobbins
- Basic and decorative thread
- Scissors, 4"
- Dressmaker shears
- Temporary adhesive spray
- Washable fabric glue
- Fray Check
- Lint roller

Fabric Selection and Preparation

Ragged-edge flowers are created with the bias-cut fabric edges left raw, so the edges fluff up when they are laundered. Fabrics with looser weaves are much better suited to this technique.

My preference for all fabric choices is 100% cotton.

I've found that these fabrics work well:
- Flannels
- Homespun
- Brushed wovens
- Osnaburg
- Printed flannels
- Yarn-dyed woven fabric

Flannel fabrics vary in weight and texture. Some are yarn-dyed, in which case both the fronts and back sides are the same color. These are most desirable for areas that are left really ragged. Quilting cottons can be used selectively for special accent pieces but are too thin and tightly woven for the major parts of a ragged-edge project.

It isn't necessary or desirable to launder the fabric. The unwashed fabric is more stable and easier to handle. Some unwashed fabrics may seem coarse and stiff. Test them by making up a block and tossing it in the washer and dryer. Most will become soft and fluffy.

Prepare the fabric by pressing out the major wrinkles. Fold with the selvedges even with one another. When working with printed fabrics, keep the unprinted selvedge area on the top side while cutting to avoid including it in the cutout.

At least two fabric patterns/colors are paired for any given project. One is for the inside and the other for the outside (which also forms the back side of the project).

Most projects utilize the same fabric in several units. Therefore, you may cut more than one layer at a time. Prepare the fabric by folding it selvedge-to-selvedge. In some cases, the fabric can be folded again with the fold placed in line with the selvedge, thereby making four layers.

For very long yardage, shorter sections may be cut to ease handling. Refer to the instructions in the chapters or projects.

The projects in the chapters use either standard size rulers for square cutouts or photocopied paper to cut out the fabric shapes. Purchased plastic templates are also available. (See Templates, page 85, for ordering information.)

For basic units, there are two fabric cutouts—one for the inside and one for the outside. Each part can be cut individually with the ruler and rotary cutter. The fabric cutouts are layered and the corners matched. When batting is inserted, it's best to cut the layers separately to allow placement of the batting between the inner and outer pieces. When the project doesn't have batting, the first fabric cutout can be layered onto the second fabric and used as a pattern. Flannel and homespun fabrics are "sticky," so the pieces don't shift during the cutting process. Since the fabrics are already matched, there is minimal handling, which in turn controls distortion of the bias edges.

Template Construction

1. Note the number of copies specified in the instructions, and photocopy the template pattern.

2. Cut along the solid lines, and join as shown in the appropriate diagram. Use the lines on your rotary mat to keep the pieces aligned.

Laura's hint

On large projects with many fabric cutouts, replace the template after it becomes tattered.

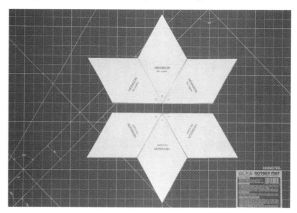

Cutting Plan

1. Spray the back side of the paper template with temporary adhesive. These sprays are designed to provide a light sticky surface. They wash out or dissipate after a short period of time.

2. Place the template on the folded fabric, set with no cut edge parallel to the grain line.

3. Cut through the two layers with a ruler and rotary cutter.

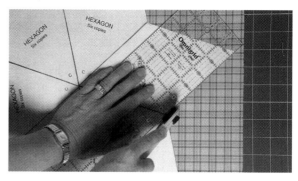

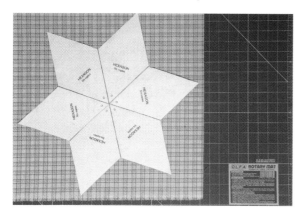

4. Repeat for the remaining pieces needed for the project.

5. For projects without batting, use a fabric cutout as a pattern. With right sides out, match an inner cutout with the outer fabric. Lay the cutout on the fabric, matching the grain lines of the cutout and the fabric. Use both the ruler and rotary cutter to cut the fabric, or cut it with scissors.

Batting

If batting is necessary (for homespun fabrics) or desired (for loftier projects), it's placed just in the center area of the unit, layered between the inside and outside fabrics. A light thin layer of batting works best. Thermore™ by Hobbs is my favorite. A very thin cotton craft-weight batting is also fine.

1. To prepare a batting template, make two photocopies of the appropriate template pattern from the appendix. Cut along the solid outer line on both copies. Match the center lines, and tape the pieces together.

2. Place the template on one or more layers of batting. A slight spritz of adhesive on the back of the template can be helpful; but don't overdo it, because it could pull the batting layers apart.

3. Cut the necessary number of batting pieces either with a ruler and rotary cutter or with scissors.

4. Layer the batting piece in the center of the fabric cutout, between the inner and outer fabric layers. In most cases, it's not necessary to baste or tack the batting, as it will be sewn into the unit in a later step.

5. Place the inner fabric cutout on top of the batting layer and match the corners. **Note: The folded points or corners will not be filled with batting.**

Folding

1. With the inner fabric facing up, fold all the points to the center of the unit so that the points meet in the center and the outer edges are evenly spaced.

2. Press the iron on the folds without smearing or pulling.

Adding Accent Colors

At this point, a third color fabric can be added to a unit by inserting a cutout under the folded flaps. Quilt cottons are an attractive choice for this piece, as the edges are sealed inside the sewn flaps. The accent cutout will be the area revealed when the petals are folded back. Small prints that contrast with the outside fabric work well.

1. Since this area will be just an outline, choose a solid-looking color for the inner folded layer that forms the petal outline. I often use a lightweight plain flannel since so little of it shows.

2. Cut out the accent fabric using the batting template. (Refer to page 10, Template Construction.)

3. Layer the cutout on top of the inner fabric under the folded flaps, so that it rests in the center.

4. Refold the flaps.

5. Topstitch ⅜" from the outer edge of the unit, so that the raw edges of the insert are encased.

Joining

There are two methods to join the ragged-edge units. There is a preferred method for each style that's determined by the shape and length of the sides. Either method may be used, but the preferred method usually holds some construction advantage.

The first method, joining by sewing in the fold, is better for units where the entire length of the units' sides meet, because it yields secure but soft seams.

In the second method, patches are sewn over zigzag-stitched joints. The topstitching and petal turn-back steps are completed before joining. This makes it easier to manipulate the units in the sewing machine. The joined seams on octagons and dodecagons are short enough that the zigzagged areas aren't stiff with stitching.

There is greater stress on ragged-edge intersections than there is with traditional quilt-joining methods. Backstitch or use the tie-down feature on your sewing machine when making or crossing any intersection.

Method One:
Joining Inside the Petal Flaps

For squares, rectangles, diamonds, triangles, and sometimes hexagons, the preferred joining method is to lift the folded petal flaps that are common to adjacent units.

1. Arrange the units as shown in the pattern.

2. Lift the flaps of two touching units.

3. Match the corners and the flaps of both units, one on top of the other, so that the fold lines are on top of one another. Pin the fold line.

4. Check the unit underneath to be sure the fold lines are even. Sew on the fold lines through both units.

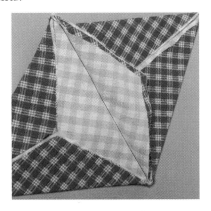

5. Continue joining groups of units into rows.

6. To join the rows together, raise the flaps of adjacent rows. Match the intersections of the previously joined units, and join in one long straight seam.

7. Stitch in the fold. As you approach the intersections, cross close to the edge just barely catching one or two threads. When crossing previously joined units, double or backstitch at the joint in the seam for security.

8. Turn and topstitch the petal areas as the joints are completed. (Review the following section on topstitching.)

9. Continue to match pairs of rows and join by sewing on the fold line between the raised flaps.

10. Topstitch the areas between the rows as you complete the joining.

11. Once all the units are joined and topstitched, skip to the binding section.

Topstitching

Topstitching the outer-edge folds and the center of the unit secures the loose flaps of the unit. For sewing through multiple layers, use a quilting needle (90/14 size).

1. Stabilize the unit with straight stitching. Sew around the outer edge of the unit at least ¼" from the edge.

2. Secure the folded points in the center of the unit by stitching over each one to form a circle.

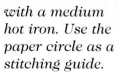

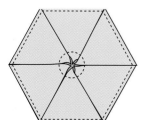

3. Cross over the beginning stitches and back tack. The distance from the center where the stitching is placed will determine the degree of fraying. A circle of 2" diameter will leave the points free to form a textured fuzzy flower center. The petal area will be shortened. Conversely, topstitching as little as ½" from the center allows for minimal center fraying and maximum petal turning.

Note that it's normal for the cut edges to migrate and not lie perfectly atop one other. This slight imperfection will be hidden or trimmed when the patches are turned and stitched.

Turning back petals

Choose the type, size, and placement of stitching that you would like for your project. The placement and type of stitching will change the appearance of the petal areas. Straight stitching close to the bias-cut petal edge will minimize shredding and leave a "wavy-lettuce" look.

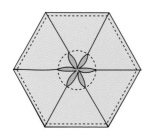

This photo shows several stitch types and placements before and after laundering.

This quilt was topstitched close to the fold, so it has quite a bit of fraying on the petal edges. The center flaps were sewn all the way to the points, so there are no loose fuzzy ends in the center.

Decorative blanket, zigzag, and hemstitching along the cut edge secure the loose threads but still leave areas to fray, depending on the stitch length and width. Satin stitching will enclose the edge, similar to machine appliqué, and eliminate the frayed look.

Using decorative and metallic threads can enhance the petal effects. Change the sewing machine needle to match the thread type.

1. Make your thread and stitch choices.

2. Turn back the fabric layers, and stitch along the folded petal flaps to reveal the inner fabric. Start at the point where the center topstitching secures the flap. Turn back the bias edges of both layers. The petal naturally bends in a tapered arc. Avoid excessive stretching, as it will distort the unit. Place your stitches either along the cut edge, centered, or along the fold, as desired.

3. Continue along all the petal edges, starting and ending in the center.

4. The turned raw edges may not line up perfectly. If the

Laura's hint

Vary the amount of turn back area within the flower to create a more natural appearance.

Make a sample block or two out of your chosen fabrics with these topstitching methods and decorative thread variations. Toss them into the washer and dryer to see what effects are produced.

underside of the fabric that shows does not match or blend well with the desired fabrics, trim away the part that peeks underneath the folded petal edges.

5. Repeat for the remaining units.

Method Two: Joining with Patches

The preferred joining method for hexagons, octagons, and dodecagons is to fill the open spaces with layered fabric patches. For all units in a project, complete the topstitching and petal turn-back steps so all the flowers are formed before joining.

1. Arrange the units in the desired pattern.

2. Join two rows of primary pieces (hexagons, octagons, or dodecagons) with zigzag stitches across the common sides of the units. In the octagon example, the four joined units form a square gap in the center and half-square triangles around the sides. (Hexagons and dodecagons have triangle-shaped gaps.) The patches are designed to cleverly and securely fill the gaps.

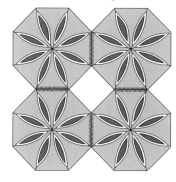

The patch fabric may match, coordinate, or contrast with the background fabric. Each choice will add a design element to the project. You may want to match the front fabric and use contrasting patches on the back side of the project. Because the back side is also attractive, consider contrasting patches to create a pattern. An especially good example is the back side of the cover quilt (shown here).

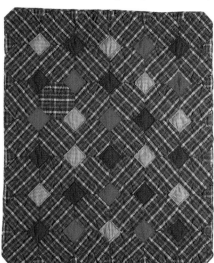

3. Cut patch pieces on the bias, using the patch template designed for the project. In each chapter, measurements and/or templates are given for the appropriate patch size and shape.

4. Place the joined group of primary pieces right side down on the work surface. Center a back side-patch over any empty space. Stitch ⅛" around the raw edges through all layers.

5. If you find the patch doesn't want to stay in place, glue-baste it in place by lifting one side of the patch and applying a small amount of washable fabric glue to the edge of the primary piece.

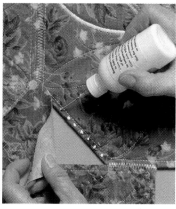

6. Repeat the application for the remaining edges of the patch. With your fingers, press the patch onto the glue.

7. Repeat the patch application steps for the remaining patches in the group.

8. Turn the project to the front side. With the batting template, cut pieces of batting that will fit inside the space between the primary pieces. (References for each template are given in each chapter.) Place a piece of batting into each open space so that it rests on top of the back side of the patch.

9. Place a front fabric patch over the batting pieces so that all the edges are evenly overlapped. Glue-baste or pin the front patches to the primary units.

10. Choose a zigzag or hemstitch on your sewing machine, and use its maximum width to secure the patches permanently to the project, stitching through all layers. Sew a test piece to check the placement of the stitching.

11. Place the patch area of the joined pieces under the presser foot so that the ridge of the primary piece rests under the sewing machine needle. Stitch along the edge of this ridge so that one swing of the zigzag or hemstitch catches the raw edge of the patch and the other stitch pierces the primary piece.

12. Stitch along the remaining sides of the patch, and continue across your first stitches to secure the patch.

Laura's hint

It's easier to manipulate a smaller joined section through the sewing machine.

13. Sew the remaining pairs of rows together, and fill the gaps with patches.

14. Add edge and corner patches as instructed in the chapter or project.

Alternate Joining Method
Joining with a modified overedge zigzag stitch

There are situations in which forming the flowers before joining the squares, rectangles, and diamonds is desirable. As more units are joined, the project becomes larger and more awkward to manage in the sewing machine. By having the units complete, all that remains is a joining step. This method also works well with octagons and dodecagons.

1. Arrange the units into the desired pattern.

2. Pick up two units that are to be joined, and place them with right sides together. Place the edges to be joined to the right side.

3. Loosen the tension slightly on your sewing machine. (I move my setting from 5 to 3.) Set the zigzag stitch width at 5.5mm and the length at 1.5mm.

4. Place the two-layered units under the needle so that the right side of the stitch falls off the edge of the fabric. The left part of the stitch should pierce all the fabric layers. Backstitch or tie off at the beginning and end of the seam.

5. Stitch along the seam line and back tack.

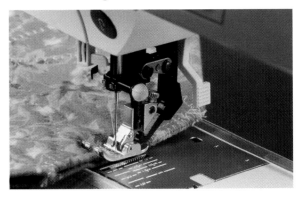

6. After completing the seam, open the units so they lie flat. If the units won't unfold, loosen the tension and stitch position. The stitches should resemble a ladder.

7. Repeat for each of the units in a row.

8. Join the remaining units into rows.

9. Place a pair of rows with right sides together, matching the intersections of the joined units. Stitch the length of the row, using the same backstitching and overedge zigzag technique.

10. Fill the gaps with layered patches (steps #3–12 of Method Two, page 15).

11. Join the pairs of rows to complete the project.

Bind and Finish

Ragged-Edge Bias Binding

1. Cut a number of 1⅛" strips of bias binding, equal to twice the combined length and width of the project, plus 20 inches.

2. Place the binding fabric on the rotary cutting mat with the selvedge even with the horizontal lines of the mat. Place a long (24") rotary ruler on the fabric so that the 45-degree line is on the selvedge. Cut along the edge of the ruler.

3. Move the ruler so that 1⅛" of fabric is under the edge. Cut along the edge of the ruler.

4. Repeat for the necessary number of strips.

5. Join the binding strips by placing the ends right sides together at a right angle, ¼" from the crossed pieces. Mark a diagonal line from the upper left intersection to the lower right intersection. Sew along the line as indicated in the photo.

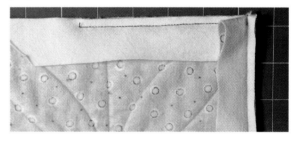

6. Trim away the fabric, leaving a ⅛" seam allowance.

7. Press the seam allowance open.

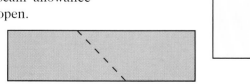

8. Place a binding strip right side down along the raw edge of the back side of the project. Place it at least six inches from any corner. Leave a three-inch tail of unsewn strip to be used later for joining.

9. Sew along the sides of the project ¼" in from the edge to exactly ¼" from the corner. Keep the strips flat and loose. Don't tug or pull while sewing.

10. Fold the binding strip open at a 45-degree angle. The right side of the binding strip will be facing up.

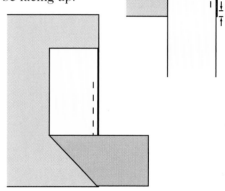

11. Refold the strip upon itself so that it turns the corner. The binding strip will be face down on the corner folds.

12. Sew the binding to the next side of the project.

13. Repeat the sewing steps for each corner.

14. On the last side, as you approach the loose tail, fold the tail right side up at a 45-degree angle.

15. Layer the ending bias strip over the angled fold of the beginning tail. Stitch over the layered bias strips.

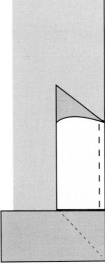

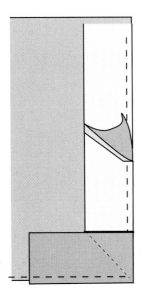

16. Trim the extra binding fabric from both strips.

17. Flip the raw edges of the binding strips to the right side, and press. Fold the binding to the front side of the project. Straighten and fold the corner areas so that the binding lies flat.

18. On the front side of the project, topstitch in the center of the strip, along the raw edge, and through all layers approximately ¼" from the fold.

Note the finished edge on the back side of the project and the raw edge on the front.

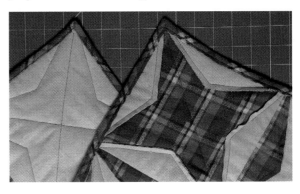

Straight-Grain Binding

Straight-grain binding may be used when there isn't sufficient fabric to cut long bias strips. By either hemstitching or serging along the front-facing edge, it can be made to look similar to the raw-edge binding.

1. Cut 1⅛" strips on the straight of grain.

2. Join the binding strips. Refer to steps #5-7, page 17.

3. Serge, hemstitch, or zigzag along one edge to stabilize the on-grain raw edge (use decorative thread).

4. With right sides together, sew the unfinished edge of the binding strip to the back side of the project where it will be encased inside the folded binding. Miter the corners as illustrated.

5. Fold the serged edge to the front of the project.

Finishing

6. Topstitch ¼" to ½" from the serged edge. Corner areas are prone to excessive raveling because of the raw edges. This is easily avoided by pressing a scant drop of Fray Check deep into the corner joints of every intersection on both the front and back sides of the project. Remove any excess by dabbing with a scrap of fabric. Dry according to the manufacturer's instructions.

1. Toss the project into the washing machine with a small amount of detergent.

2. Rinse twice.

3. Tumble dry in the clothes dryer.

Laura's hint

Check the lint trap often during the drying process, and remove the excess lint.

4. Once the project is dry, shake it out to further fluff the ragged edges.

Squiggly 2 Squares

Basic Squares

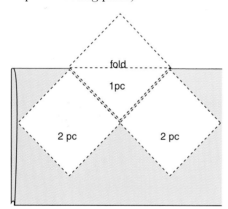

When you learn of the imminent birth of a new baby, make a cuddly baby blanket quickly with this super-easy technique. Choose two colors of flannel and a lightweight batting. Cut the squares on the bias, fold, join, and topstitch. With a quick round of binding, you're finished!

For an easy group project or for teaching a beginning quilter, this is a big confidence builder.

Fabric Selection and Preparation:
Choose loose-woven fabrics, such as homespun, flannel, plaid shirtings, or osnaburg. Contrast the inner and outer fabric colors. Using a neutral or texture for the inner fabric will set off the petal areas.

Template:
12½" square rotary ruler

Cutting Plan:
Cut equal numbers of 12½" bias squares from two different fabrics. (See illustration below for a bias-square cutting plan.)

fold

1pc

2 pc   2 pc

Assembly:
1. Place an inside square on an outside square with the right sides out.
2. Find the center of the squares by alternately folding the corners to the center and finger pressing a cross.

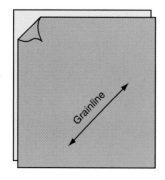

Grainline

3. Fold all four of the two-layered corners to the center. Press the folds. Note that the folds follow the straight grain.

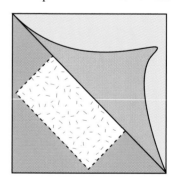

Batting:
1. If batting is necessary or desired, open the pressed squares. Insert an 8" square of batting diagonally centered between the layers of folded squares.
2. The 8" square may appear to be too small, but the bulk of the two fabric squares "eats up" some of the fabric in the folding.
3. Refold the flaps to the center of the square.

Joining:
1. Arrange the square units according to your plan—three rows of four units, six rows of four units, etc.

2. Join the squares by opening the touching flaps. Match the corners and fold lines. Check that the fold on the underside is matched to the top. Pin along the fold line.

3. Sew on the fold line through both layers. Be careful not to rearrange the two layers of fabric and batting.

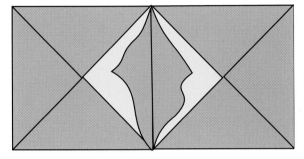

4. Join the squares into rows. Turn back and topstitch the petals of the joined flaps.

Topstitching:
Secure the loose flaps by topstitching in a straight line through the middle of the joined units.

Forming Petals:
1. Choose the type, size, and placement of stitching for the petal turn-back area. Refer to the Topstitching section in Chapter One (page 13).

2. Sew three to five stitches on the folded flap to secure the corners, turn back the cut edges of the petal on a curve, and topstitch through all the layers. Finish by flattening the petal fabric for three to five stitches from the end.

3. Repeat for the joined units in the row.

4. Alternate joining the units together, topstitching, and turning back the petals.

5. Once the units are joined in rows, join the rows together.

6. Continue topstitching the joined areas of the rows.

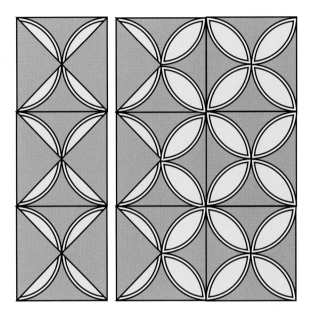

7. Bind the outer edge with a single layer of bias-cut binding fabric.

Finishing:
1. Apply a scant drop of Fray Check deep into the joined corners on the back and front sides of the quilt. Let dry.

2. Toss in the washer and dryer, and fluff.

Squares can also be joined, after topstitching the petals, with a modified overedge zigzag stitch (page 16).

Purple Posies

This lavender quilt is reminiscent of grandma's house. Alternate cute little flower prints with textured solids for the inside and outside pieces. Use this nine-block project for a table centerpiece, wall hanging, or antimacassar.

Finished size: 25" square
Difficulty level: Easiest
Block size: 8½" square

Fabric requirements:
Marcus Brothers Flannels
   1 yard small floral print
   1 yard light purple
   1 yard dark purple print
   1 yard medium purple print

Binding:
Included in the medium purple print

Templates:
12½" square rotary ruler

Cutting Plan:
In the quantity specified, cut 12½" bias squares from each of the fabrics. Refer to Cutting Plan (page 20) for the cutting diagram.
   5 small-floral print
   5 light purple

   4 dark-purple print
   4 medium-purple print
   3 medium-purple print, 1⅛" wide x 42" long bias binding strips

Layout:
Arrange three rows of three squares.

Specific Instructions:
Mix and match the light, medium, and dark fabrics as shown in the photo.

Binding:
Join the 1⅛" wide bias binding strips, and stitch them to the project with the raw edge on the front side.

Finishing:
1. Apply a scant drop of Fray Check deep into the joined corners on the back and front sides of the quilt. Let dry.
2. Toss in the washer and dryer, and fluff.

Crinkly Blanket

Finished size: 36" x 45"
Difficulty level: Easy
Block size: 9"

Fabric requirements:
Flannels
   3½ yards yellow
   4 yards pink plaid

Binding:
Included in the pink plaid fabric

Template:
12½" standard rotary ruler

Cutting Plan:
Refer to Cutting Plan (page 20) for the bias-square cutting diagram.
   20 yellow 12½" bias-cut squares
   20 pink plaid 12½" bias-cut squares
   5 pink plaid 1⅛" wide bias binding strips

Layout:
Arrange four rows of five units.

Specific Instructions:
Alternate the pink and yellow plaids, as the inner and outer fabrics, in a checkerboard style.

Binding:
1. Join the 1⅛" wide bias binding strips, and sew right sides together on the back side of the quilt.
2. Fold to the front, and sew along the raw edge.

Finishing:
1. Apply a scant drop of Fray Check deep into the joined corners on the back and front sides of the quilt. Let dry.
2. Toss in the washer and dryer, and fluff.

Pink and yellow plaids dance over this squishy-soft baby blanket. It's one of the easiest quilts to make. Simply cut, fold, join, and topstitch the squares.

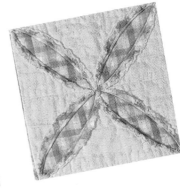

Wrinkles in Red

    I kept putting off making this quilt, because the fabric I chose seemed "muddy." It was originally purchased for a jacket, but I decided to recycle it. After procrastinating for months, I did get the job done and was delighted.

    Mix and match many like-colored plaids. Don't shy away from the very bright or the dull flannels. Fabrics that mimic comfy shirts work well along with a creamy light flannel for the petals.

Finished size: 50" x 60"
Difficulty level: Easiest
Block size: 8¾"

Fabric requirements:
Inner Petals
   8 yards cream brushed flannel
Mixed outer fabrics of brushed homespun
   2½ yards bright red check
   3½ yards large red plaid
   2½ yards small red plaid
2 yards 45" wide lightweight batting

Binding:
Mixed scraps

Templates:
12½" square rotary ruler

Cutting Plan:
Refer to Cutting Plan (page 20) for the bias-square cutting diagram.

42 cream 12½" bias squares
13 bright red check 12½" bias squares
16 large red plaid 12½" bias squares
13 small red plaid 12½" bias squares
7 bias cut 1⅛" wide binding strips of mixed
   scraps
42 batting squares, 7¾" x 7¾"

Layout:
Arrange the 42 folded squares in six rows of seven units, randomly mixing light, medium, and bright plaids.

Binding:
Join the binding strips, and stitch with the raw edge folded to the front.

Finishing:
1. Apply a scant drop of Fray Check deep into the joined corners on the back and front sides of the quilt. Let dry.
2. Toss in the washer and dryer, and fluff.

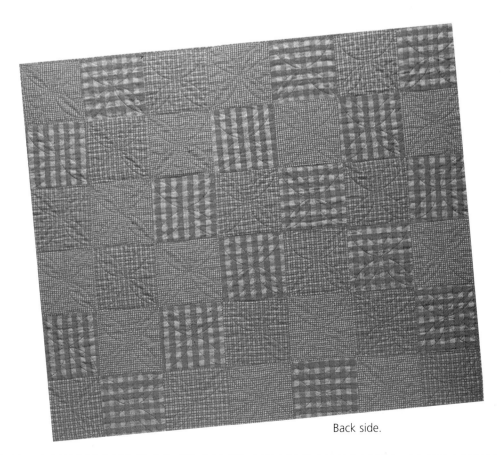

Back side.

Peek-a-Boo Squares

Just like the basic squiggles, this peek-a-boo version is quick and easy. With heavier flannels, there's no need for batting. Instead a third layer of fabric is inserted to "peek" through the petals as a third color or pattern. The inner square fabric forms an accent that outlines the petal area. The fabric insert can be pieced into a four patch. Use many scraps for variety. The insert fabric can be flannel or a basic cotton calico.

Cutting Plan:

Refer to Cutting Plan (page 20) for the bias-square cutting diagram.

1. Cut equal numbers of 12½" bias squares from two different fabrics.

2. Place one inside square on an outside square with right sides out.

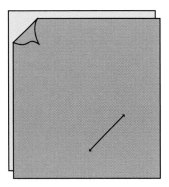

3. Find the center of the squares by alternately folding the corners to the center and finger pressing a cross.

4. Fold all four of the two-layered corners to the center. Press the folds. Note that the folds follow the straight grain.

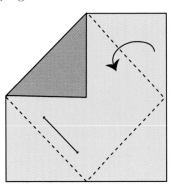

Accent squares:

1. Cut 8" squares of inner accent fabric on the straight of grain. These squares seem too small, but the bulk from folding the layered fabric squares "eats up" some of the fabric.

2. Unfold the pressed square, and lay the 8" fabric square centered on the inner fabric. Refold the square.

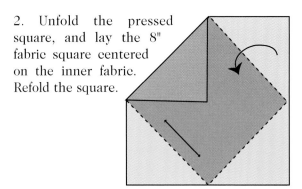

Note: *Batting is unnecessary because of the extra accent layer.*

Joining:

While joining these units, be careful not to disturb the unattached accent squares when lifting the flaps as instructed in Step 2.

1. Arrange the square units according to your plan—three rows of four units, six rows of four units, etc.

2. Join the squares by opening the touching flaps. Match the corners and fold lines. Check that the fold on the underside is matched to the top. Pin along the fold line.

3. Sew on the fold line through both layers. Be careful not to rearrange the two layers of fabric and the accent square.

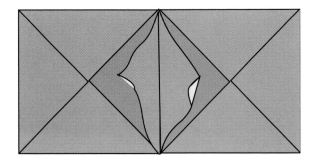

Topstitching:
Secure the loose flaps by topstitching in a straight line through the middle of the joined units.

Forming Petals:
1. Choose the type, size, and placement stitching for the petal turn-back area. Refer to the Topstitching section in Chapter One (page 13).
2. Sew three to five stitches on the folded flap to secure the corners, turn back the cut edges of the petal on a curve, and topstitch through all the layers. Finish by flattening the petal fabric for three to five stitches from the end.
3. Repeat for the joined units in the row.
4. Alternate joining the units together, topstitching, and turning back the petals.
5. Once the units are joined in rows, join the rows together.

6. Continue topstitching the joined areas of the rows.

7. Bind the outer edge with a single layer of bias-cut binding fabric.

Finishing:
1. Apply a scant drop of Fray Check deep into the joined corners on the back and front sides of the quilt. Let dry.
2. Toss in the washer and dryer, and fluff.

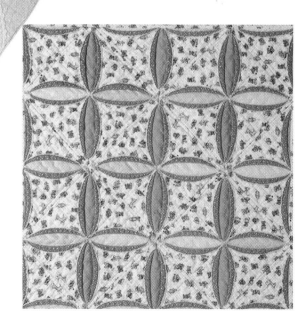

Checkerboard Peek-a-Boo Option

Substitute four-color checkerboard inserts for the accent square to create a fun color variation.

1. Prepare the insert by cutting one 4¾" strip from four different fabrics.
2. With right sides together, sew two strips with a ¼" seam allowance along the long edge.
3. Repeat for the other two strips.
4. Cross cut 4¾" sections from both paired strips.
5. With the center seams matched and right sides together, sew one of each of the cross cut pairs to form a four patch square. Press the seams open.
6. Insert this checkerboard square inside the folded unit. The square will measure 8½" square. If it seems too large when the flaps are folded back, trim it to 8¼" square.

7. Turn back and topstitch the petals.
8. Join the units with the modified overedge zigzag method (page 16).

Finishing:
1. Apply a scant drop of Fray Check deep into the joined corners on the back and front sides of the quilt. Let dry.
2. Toss in the washer and dryer, and fluff.

Pastel Peeking Checkerboard

Finished size: 21½" square
Difficulty level: Easy
Block size: 8" square

Fabric requirements:
Marcus Brother's flannel
   1½ yards white baby print
   1½ yards blue tiny print
   4¾" pink selvedge-to-selvedge strip
   4¾" lavender selvedge-to-selvedge strip
   4¾" green selvedge-to-selvedge strip
   4¾" yellow selvedge-to-selvedge strip

Binding:
Included in the white baby print

Templates:
12½" square rotary ruler

Cutting Plan:
Cut eight 12½" bias squares from the white baby print and the blue print flannel.
3 white baby print 1⅛" wide straight cut binding strips.

Specific Instructions:
1. Refer to the photo on page 27 and the Checkerboard Peek-a-Boo Option instructions on the previous page. Prepare eight four-patch insert squares from the four 4¾" selvedge-to-selvedge strips.
2. Three units are cut to set the blocks on point. Cut two completed units in half on the diagonal. Insert these halves on the top and sides to fill in the triangular areas.
3. Cut the third unit into four pieces by cutting diagonally in both directions.

Construction:
1. Layer the four-patch squares on top of the blue inner squares, under the folded flaps.
2. Refold, turn, and topstitch the flaps.
3. Join using the modified overedge zigzag method described in the Joining section of Chapter One (page 16).

Binding:
1. Join the binding strips.

Sweet baby prints "peek" around the petals of this small baby wall quilt. Setting the squares on point creates a different variation from the usual basic square. This too is a quick and easy quilt that can be stitched in time for the next baby shower.

2. Complete the binding as instructed in the Straight-Grain Binding section, page 18.

Finishing:
1. Apply a scant drop of Fray Check deep into the joined corners on the back and front sides of the quilt. Let dry.
2. Toss in the washer and dryer, and fluff.

Starry Squares

These twisty stars are so simple! Start with octagon-shaped pieces, fold the points toward the center, and you've got a sparkling quilt! This pattern lends itself to pretty embroidery patterns and special accents. Alternate the inner and outer fabrics in checkerboard fashion to create an optical illusion. The blue and green project on page 34 uses this arrangement. An overlay of fancy lace yields a "windowpane" effect.

Try lace overlay or add your own embellishments.

Template preparation:

1. Make two photocopies of the octagon-shaped starry square template on page 85.
2. Cut along the outer lines.
3. Match the center lines, and tape the two pieces together.

Fabric selection and preparation:

1. Fold the fabric selvedge-to-selvedge, and then fold again, matching the fold to the selvedge.
2. Place the paper template on the folded outer fabric, rotated so that all cut edges are on the bias.

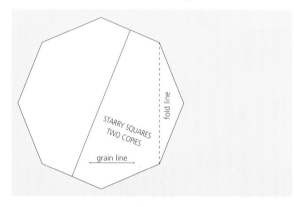

※ ※ *Laura's* hint

If your fabric has a plaid pattern, use the stripes to arrange the template. Place the fold lines with the grain, and the cut edges will be bias.

3. Place a rotary ruler with its edge on top of the template edge.
4. Cut along the template edges through all four layers of fabric. You will have four fabric octagons.
5. Repeat for the number of pieces needed for your project.
6. Repeat the process using the inner fabric.

Batting:

The starry square design has a large open center area that requires batting.

1. Cut 7¼" squares of batting.
2. Place a square of batting on the wrong side of the outer fabric octagon so that it is aligned with the straight grain of the octagon.
3. With its right side up, place an inner fabric octagon over the batting, rotating it to match the grain line and corners.

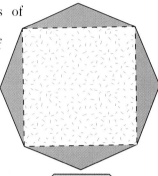

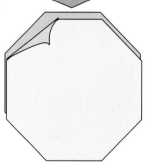

Folding:

1. Fold the corners on the straight of grain.
2. Form a square.

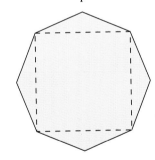

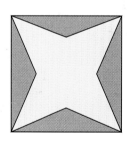

※ ※ *Laura's* hint

When pressing the points along the fold lines, exaggerate the folds toward the center to create an approximately ¹⁄₁₆" overlap at the corners. The intersections will have a bit more fabric to catch in the joining step and will be more stable.

Joining:

1. Arrange your units according to the project instructions. The units are sewn together in rows.
2. Open the folded flaps of two adjacent units.

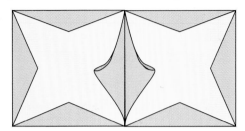

3. Match the fold lines and pin.
4. Sew in the fold.
5. Open the units and refold the flaps back to their respective units.

Topstitching:

1. With the flaps folded flat, topstitch the pointed flaps that have been joined.

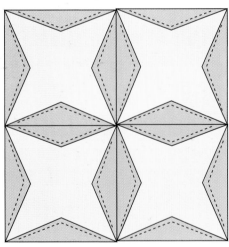

2. Repeat the joining and topstitching steps for the remaining units in the row.
3. Once all rows are joined, line up two rows side by side. Open the row of flaps between the rows to be joined. Match the joints and the adjacent fold lines. Pin across the folds.
4. Sew the two rows together by stitching in the fold.
5. Back stitch over the intersections to reinforce them.
6. Press the flaps back to their original unit. Topstitch the flaps.
7. Repeat with the remaining rows.

Quilting:

Topstitch diagonally across the center of the squares in both directions to form an "X" quilting pattern.

Binding:

Refer to the Bind and Finish section in Chapter One (page 17) for instructions on how to bind the project.

1. Bind with joined single layer bias-cut fabric strips.
2. Note that the corners formed at the intersections may bow out a bit. As you apply the binding, trim the corners (a scant ¼") even with the sides of the project.

Finishing:

1. Apply a scant drop of Fray Check deep into the joined corners on the back and front sides of the quilt. Let dry.
2. Toss in the washer and dryer. Check the lint trap often and remove excess lint.

This wall hanging's special effect is an overlay of embroidered curtain fabric.

$\mathcal{D}$ad's $\mathcal{P}$laid $\mathcal{S}$hirt

Finished size: 43" x 57"
Difficulty level: Easy
Block size: 7" square

Fabric requirements:
Homespun
   4½ yards blue check
   4 yards green plaid
1¾ yards 45" wide lightweight
   batting

Binding:
Included in blue check fabric

Templates:
Starry Square octagon-
   shaped template, 2 copies
   page 85
OR
Purchased plastic octagon
   template (see Templates,
   page 85, for ordering
   instructions)

Cutting Plan:
48 blue plaid octagons
48 green plaid octagons
6 blue check 1⅛" bias binding
   strips
48 batting squares, 6½" x 6½"

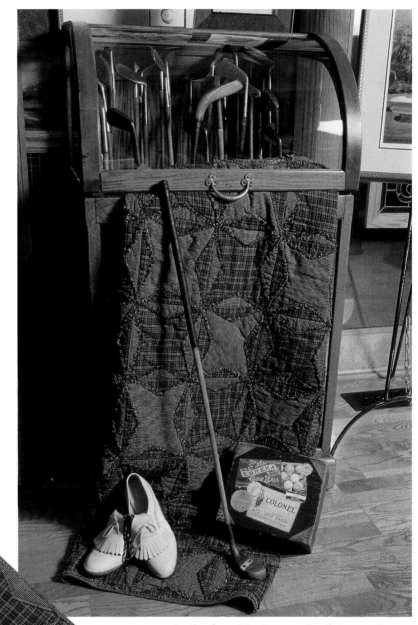

I made the four-block sample of this quilt and thought the design would resemble a fleur-de-lis. On a lark, I decided to mix the inner and outer fabrics checkerboard style. Once completed, to my surprise, circles popped out! These homespun plaids are very light and soft. For a heavier version, use brushed flannel.

Layout:
6 rows of 8 blocks

Special Instructions:
Stitch diagonally across all the square units to secure the batting.

Binding:
Bind with 1⅛" joined bias strips, stitched with the raw edge on the front of the quilt.

Curly Blue Rings

Finished size: 44" x 60"
Difficulty level: Easy
Block size: 7¼" square

Fabric requirements:
45" wide flannel
4½ yards purple plaid
4 yards blue brushed flannel
1¾ yard 45" wide lightweight batting

Binding:
Included in the purple plaid fabric

Templates:
Starry Square octagonal-shaped template, 2 copies page 85
OR
Purchased plastic octagon template (see Templates, page 85, for ordering instructions)

Cutting Plan:
48 purple plaid octagons
48 blue flannel octagons
6 purple plaid 1⅛" x 44" bias binding strips
48 batting squares, 6¾" x 6¾"

Layout:
Alternate the plaid and baby blue flannel in six rows of eight blocks.

Special Instructions:
Stitch diagonally across all the square units to secure the batting.

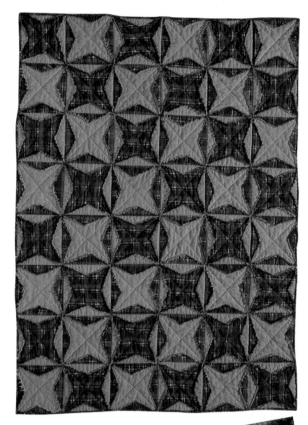

This is a heavier version of the alternated checkerboard arrangement, using brushed flannel. The plain blocks make a perfect canvas for your embroidery stitches. Or, make a pattern in quilting stitches to secure the batting layer.

Binding:
Bind with 1⅛" joined bias strips, stitched with the raw edge on the front of the quilt.

Finishing:
1. Apply a scant drop of Fray Check deep into the joined corners on the back and front sides of the quilt. Let dry.
2. Toss in the washer and dryer, and fluff.

3 Wrinkly Rectangles

Basic Rectangle

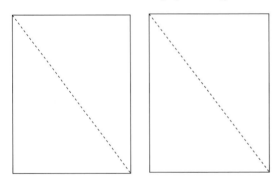

These are just as easy as their cousins, the squares! There's an advantage, however, because you get more quilt for your fabric, and that's good! The large template is made to just fit between the selvedge and the fold of 45" wide fabrics. Therefore, when the diamond shapes are cut, most of the fabric goes into the quilt. Because they're elongated, the units form different patterns.

As with other projects based on four sides to the unit, rectangles are really easy to construct. Colors can be alternated checkerboard style, mixed and matched, or kept to just two choices.

They also can be matched with other shapes in this book for even more variety.

Template Construction:

1. On two 8½" x 11" sheets of plain paper, draw a line from the upper left corner to the lower right corner. Cut the two sheets of paper along the lines.

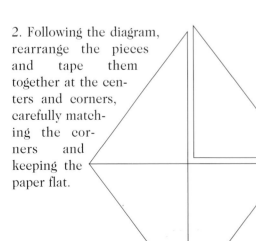

2. Following the diagram, rearrange the pieces and tape them together at the centers and corners, carefully matching the corners and keeping the paper flat.

Fabric Selection and Preparation:

1. Choose fabrics for the inner and outer layers.
2. Fold the fabric selvedge-to-selvedge.

Cutting Plan:

1. Place the template on the fabric with the center lines following the grain.

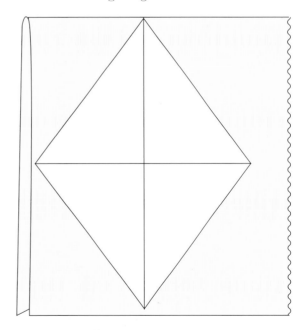

2. With temporary adhesive, spray baste the template onto the fabric.
3. Place a rotary ruler on top of the template so that the edge of the ruler lines up with the edge of the template.

4. With a rotary cutter at the edge of the ruler, cut just to each corner of the template. Avoid over-cutting, as you will ruin the next piece.

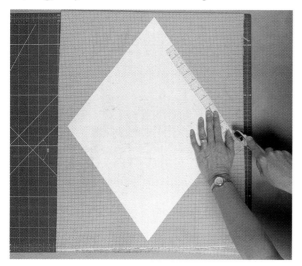

5. Remove the two diamond fabric pieces.
6. Place the template on the uncut fabric along the grain line, leaving approximately an inch between the cutout area and the template.

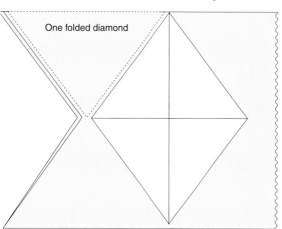

One folded diamond

7. Repeat steps #4-6.
8. Unfold the leftover fabric triangle, found between the two pairs of diamonds that were just cut. Press to remove the fold lines.
9. With the template, cut another single fabric diamond.
10. Repeat the cutting for the inner and outer fabrics.

Assembly:
Place an inner fabric diamond on an outer fabric diamond with wrong sides together, matching the corners.

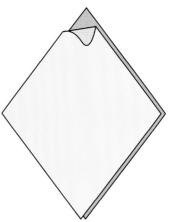

Batting:
1. To add a batting layer, cut 8" x 10½" rectangles of batting.
2. Layer the batting rectangle centered between the inner and outer fabric layers.

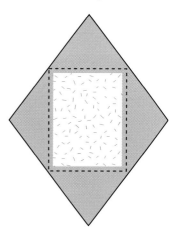

Folding:
1. Find the center of the inside fabric diamond by folding the piece in half and finger-pressing at the fold line. Repeat in the other direction to form a cross.
2. With the two layers together, fold each corner to

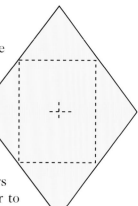

the center, matching the points to the cross formed by the folds.

3. Press the rectangle flat, carefully forming the outer corners by butting the raw edges against each other, right up to the corner.

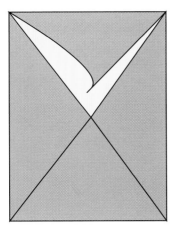

Joining:

1. Arrange the pressed rectangles in the pattern shown in the project or according to your own design.

2. Join rows by opening adjacent flaps of units and sewing on the fold. (Refer to the joining section of Chapter One, page 12.)

3. Once a row is joined, topstitch the flaps into petals by folding back the raw edges along a curve and stitching through all the fabric layers.

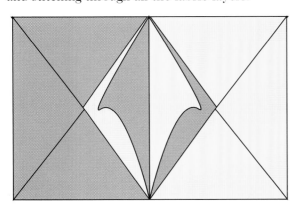

4. Join the rows and topstitch as you go.

Binding:

Once the quilt is fully assembled, bind with a single layer of 1⅛" strips of bias binding, with the raw edge folded to the front.

Finishing:

1. Apply a scant drop of Fray Check deep into the joined corners on the back and front sides of the quilt. Let dry.

2. Toss in the washer and dryer, and fluff.

Punctuated Placemats and Napkins

These placemats can be made from any loose-weave fabrics. They are very elegant when made up in linen. For casual meals, flannels are thick and cushiony. Add an accent layer for pizzazz.

Finished size: 11" x 17"
Difficulty level: Easy
Block size: 8½" x 11"

Fabric requirements:
2 yards dark red
3 yards light red (1 yard for four napkins)

Binding:
Included in the dark red fabric

Templates:
Rectangle template—2 sheets of paper, 8½" x 11"
(see Template Construction, page 37)

Cutting Plan:
8 dark red rectangles
8 light red rectangles
5 dark red 1⅛" wide bias-cut strips

Specific Instructions:
Alternate the dark and light fabrics for the inner and outer layers.

Binding:
Join the 1⅛" bias-edge binding strips. Stitch with the raw edge folded to the front.

Bonus

Use the triangle-shaped cutoffs to make coasters.

1. Cut four 6½" bias squares from both fabrics.

2. Cut four 4" squares from both fabrics.

3. Layer a 4" square set diagonally on a contrasting 6½" square.

4. Fold the corners to the center, turn the petal edges, and topstitch.

Finishing:

Toss in the washer and dryer, and fluff.

"Xs" and "Os"

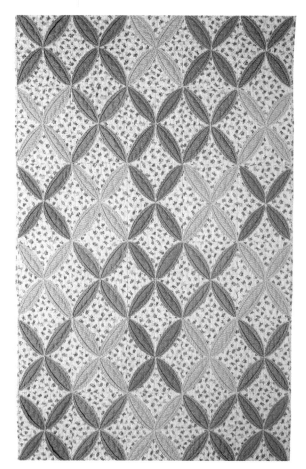

These reproduction print flannels combine to make a sweet baby blanket. Add more variety to the petal colors for a scrappy look.

Finished size: 40" x 64"
Difficulty level: Easy
Block size: 8" x 10"

Fabric requirements:
Marcus Brother's flannel
    8 yards white baby print
    2½ yards green print
    2½ yards yellow print
    2½ yards blue print

Binding:
Included in the white baby print

Template:
Rectangle template—2 sheets of paper, 8½" x 11" (see Template Construction, page 37)

Cutting Plan:
30 white baby print rectangles
10 green print rectangles
10 yellow print rectangles
10 blue print rectangles
6 white baby print 1⅛" wide bias binding strips

Layout:
5 rows of 6 blocks

Specific Instructions:
1. Prepare the rectangles per the instructions starting on page 37.
2. Arrange the colors in the project pattern.

Binding:
Join the 1⅛" bias-edge binding strips. Stitch with the raw edge folded to the front.

Accented Rectangle

A third accent color can be added in the petal reveal area by inserting an 8¼" x 10¾" rectangle of fabric between the inner fabric and the folded flaps. Note the accent petal reveal color in the upper placemat.

1. Cut 8¼" x 10¾" rectangles. *Note: The rectangles may be too large when heavier fabrics are used. In that case, trim the rectangles to 8" x 10½".*
2. Lift the flaps of the folded rectangles. Center the insert on the inner fabric layer.
3. Topstitch ⅜" in from the outer folded edge to secure the inserted fabric rectangle.
4. Turn back and topstitch the petals.
5. Join with a modified overedge zigzag stitch (page 16).

Dazzling Diamonds 4

Basic Diamond

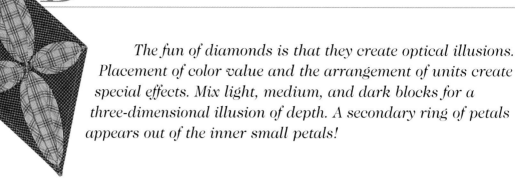

The fun of diamonds is that they create optical illusions. Placement of color value and the arrangement of units create special effects. Mix light, medium, and dark blocks for a three-dimensional illusion of depth. A secondary ring of petals appears out of the inner small petals!

Template Construction:
1. Make two photocopies of the diamond template on page 86.
2. Cut along the outer solid line of both copies.
3. Join the halves to form the template.

Fabric Selection and Preparation:
A project will have fabrics designated for the inner area that form the petal reveal. For illusions, keep the inner fabric the same throughout the project. A neutral inner fabric will focus attention on the pattern of the outer blocks. The outer fabric will surround the flowers and form the back side of the project. Coordinating light, medium, and dark prints will create the dimensional illusion.

Cutting Plan:
All fabric edges will be cut on the bias to minimize shredding.

Option One: Cut the pieces from the outer fabric(s) with the paper template. Each of these outside fabric cutouts will be placed on the piece of inner fabric that you have paired with it. The outside fabric cutout will serve as a pattern when cutting the inner fabric with a rotary cutter or scissors. The two layers are perfectly matched and ready for the folding step.

Option Two: For projects with batting, cut all the fabric using the paper template with either scissors or with the rotary ruler and cutter. The piece of batting is placed on the outer piece, and the inner piece is layered over it, matching the points. The layered pieces are then folded to form the diamonds.

For Both Options:
1. Begin by cutting the outer fabric using the paper template.

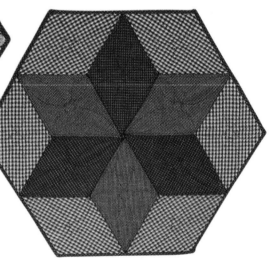

The backs of these quilts are just as intriguing as the fronts.

2. Fold the outside fabric(s) selvedge-to-selvedge, forming two layers.

3. Spray the back side of the paper template with temporary adhesive spray.

4. Place the template on one of the folded fabrics, so the grain line marking is perpendicular to the selvedge.

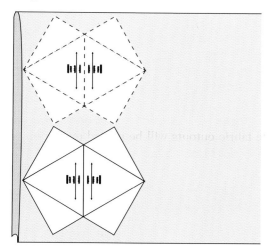

Cutting plan:

1. Place a rotary ruler on the template, aligning the edge of the ruler with an outer line of the paper template.

2. Use a rotary cutter to cut through both layers of fabric along the edge of the ruler. Cut just to the inner corners. (Olfa's rotary point cutter is handy for precise cutting of the inner corners.) Cutting past the corner will weaken the seams.

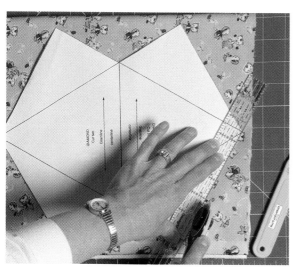

3. Move the ruler around the template and repeat the cutting until the entire piece is cut out. Folded fabric will yield two pieces. As an alternative, while being careful to keep the template in place, you can cut the fabric with scissors.

Cutting the Inner Fabric:

If you are working with long yardage, you may wish to cut the inner fabric into one-yard lengths to make it more manageable.

1. Fold the fabric selvedge-to-selvedge, forming two layers.

2. Place an outer fabric cutout on an inner fabric piece, wrong sides together, matching the grain lines.

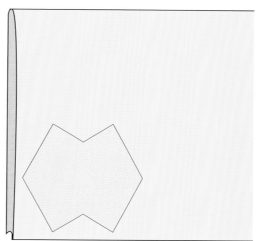

3. Using the cutout piece as the pattern, cut the inner fabric layer with a rotary cutter and ruler. The cut pieces are now perfectly layered and ready to fold. (Remove the second inner cutout and match it to another outer piece.)

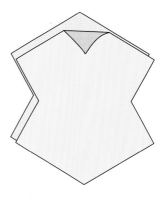

Batting (Inserting Batting Cutouts):

1. To prepare a batting template, make a photocopy of the diamond batting template on page 87. Cut along the solid line.

2. Use this template to cut thin lightweight batting (Hobbs Thermore is ideal) with a ruler and rotary cutter into diamond-shaped pieces. (Refer to the Batting section in Chapter One, page 11.)

3. Place a diamond-shaped piece of batting centered between the inner and outer fabric cutouts.

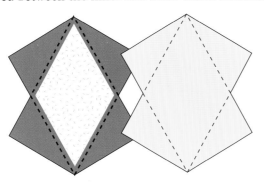

4. Continue with the folding instructions. *Note: There is no need to secure the batting at this point, as it will be sewn to the unit later, in the topstitching step.*

Folding:

Fold the points of the piece to the center, forming a diamond.

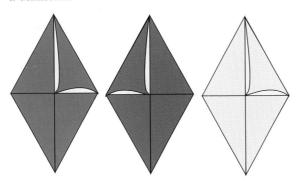

Joining:

Joining a group of diamonds is easier to manage than joining the whole project at once.

1. Arrange your diamond units in the desired pattern.

2. The preferred (but not necessarily the easiest) method of joining diamonds is to raise the petal flaps of adjacent units and sew in the fold. To keep the pattern organized, join units in groups of three (two vertical and one horizontal) units.

Edge units:

1. Cut whole units in half horizontally or vertically to fill in and square up the sides of a project. Incorporate these half-size pieces into the rows at the outer edges of the project.

2. Join the medium and dark units with a vertical seam.

3. Open the flaps that touch, match the fold lines, and sew in the fold.

4. Join the light unit across the top of the two previously joined units.

5. Open a flap on the light unit and one on the dark unit. Match the fold lines and pin.

6. Stitch on the fold line from the center to the outer edge.

7. Open the other flap of the light unit, and match it to the top flap of the medium unit. Match the fold lines. Stitch from the center to the outer edge.

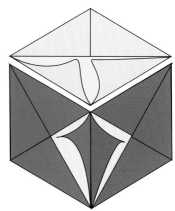

8. Repeat for the remaining block units in the row.

Forming Petals:

Turn back the raw edges of the joined folded flaps to form petals. Topstitch along the edge, either with straight or decorative stitching. The placement of the stitching line will determine the degree of fray after laundering. Straight stitching ⅛" from the raw edge will have less fraying than stitching ¼" away. Zigzag, blanket, or hemstitching will decrease the amount of fray by securing more of the raw edges and forming a ridged wavy area, outlining the petals.

Joining the rows:

1. Join the three-unit blocks between the medium and dark intersections to make a row. Topstitch the petals as you complete the joints. *Note: Blocks may be joined in other combinations for different optical illusions. Refer to the example on page 44.*

2. Repeat for the desired number of rows.

3. The joining seam between the rows zigzags back and forth along the edge of the joined blocks. Lift the flaps of the units along the bottom and top of the rows to be joined. Match the intersections of the first block, and pin. Pin along the fold line of the matched flaps. Check the underneath layer to be sure that the pins are centered in the fold.

4. Sew in the folds. Back tack at the intersections.

5. Repeat for each of the units along the row. The stitching line will alternate directions with the lines of the diamonds.

6. Turn back and topstitch the petal areas of the joined seam.

Binding:

Refer to the Bind and Finish section in Chapter One, page 17.

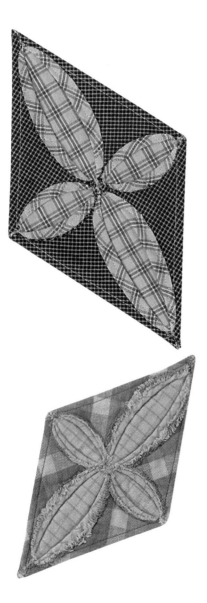

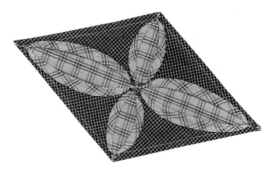

Swirling and Tumbling Blocks

12 light green diamonds
12 medium green diamonds
12 dark green diamonds
4 dark green 1¼" wide bias binding strips

There's an optical illusion here! Baby blocks appear with circulating petals. The back side is the familiar "tumbling blocks" pattern shown at right. Soften the look with pastels for a cute baby blanket. Sharpen it up with primary colors.

Finished size: 34" x 40"
Difficulty level: Intermediate
Block size: 6½" x 11"

Fabric requirements:
Marcus Brother's Flannel
   3 yards butter yellow
   1 yard light green
   1 yard medium green
   1 yard dark green

Binding:
Included in the dark green fabric

Templates:
Diamond template, 2 copies page 86

Cutting Plan
36 butter yellow diamonds

Specific Instructions:
Five light green units will be cut to fill in the edge areas. ***Note:*** *The light diamonds are set so the longer side is horizontal.*
1. Cut three light green units in half horizontally. These halves will be long and narrow. Use these halves for the top and bottom rows.
2. Cut two light green units in half vertically. These halves will be equilateral triangles. Place these halves at the ends of three rows to fill in the space and "square" up the sides.

Binding:
After the units are joined, bind with the bias-edge strips. Stitch with the raw edge folded to the front of the project.

Finishing:
1. Apply a scant drop of Fray Check deep into the joined corners on the back and front sides of the quilt. Let dry.
2. Toss in the washer and dryer, and fluff.

Twisty 5 Triangles

Basic Triangle

Triangles are so much fun because their petals can be folded back in multiple designs. Some are flowery, and some are more geometric. They're all very simple! Because the units are smaller, they're easy to manage. With as few as six units, you can make a centerpiece. Add on for a table runner, baby blanket, or sofa throw.

Like their geometric relatives in this book, triangles are cut from one shape and folded into another. Hexagon cutouts fold into triangles. Edges are cut on the bias, and the cut fabric edges are folded back to reveal the inner fabric color and to form the curved petal shapes. However, if the edges are folded diagonally, a star pattern is formed.

Play around with several designs. These make wonderful gifts.

Template Preparation:
1. Make two photocopies of the triangle template on page 88, and cut along the lines.
2. Tape the two halves together and make a hexagon-shaped template.

Fabric Selection and Preparation:
1. Select two or more fabrics with coordinating or contrasting colors. Placement of the inner and outer fabrics dramatically changes the final design.

2. Review the design options shown in this chapter's photos. Designate the fabric for the inner and outer layers.
3. Fold the fabrics selvedge-to-selvedge, and fold again, matching the fold to the selvedge and creating four layers.

Left: In this quilt, all the units are made with the same light outer fabric and dark inner fabric.

Right: In this quilt, the pattern is the same, but the dark and light fabrics are alternated in every other unit, producing a completely different look.

Cutting plan:

1. Place the hexagon-shaped template on the folded fabric, being careful to orient the template using the "grain line" marking. Edges are bias cut to facilitate turning back the petals and to create the "lettuce-edge" effect.

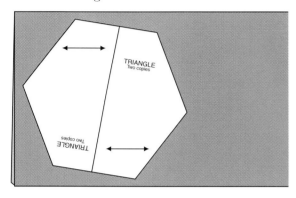

2. Place a rotary ruler with the edge on top of the cut template edge.
3. Cut along the ruler edge through all four layers, using the rotary cutter.
4. You will have four pieces. Repeat until you have the total number of pieces you need for your project. *Note: If you are making the two-color, six-unit centerpiece, cut just two layers for the second set of each fabric.*
5. Repeat this procedure with the other fabric(s).

Assembly:

1. For projects without batting, layer the inner and outer fabrics with the right side of the fabrics on the outside. Place one hexagon-shaped piece of inside fabric on top of a hexagon of outside fabric, matching the straight edges and points.

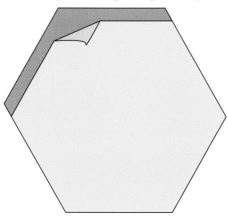

2. Fold three alternate corners to the center, adjusting the cut edges so they lie flat while matching the points in the center to form a triangle.
3. Press.

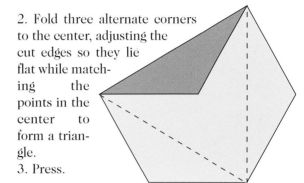

Batting:

Add a layer of batting for projects that are made from thinner homespun fabric or to create a thicker padded project.

1. Prepare a batting template by making a photocopy of the batting template on page 89. Cut along the solid line of the triangle.
2. Place the batting template on one or more layers of batting.
3. Using a ruler and rotary cutter, cut the layer(s) of batting along the edge of the template.
4. Insert the triangle of batting between the inner and outer la   ly centering it so that no edg   f the fabric.

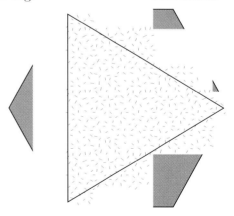

5. Fold three alternate corners to the center, adjusting the cut edges so they lie flat while matching the points in the center to form a triangle.
6. Prepare the remaining units by repeating the layering, pressing, and batting steps.

Joining:

1. Arrange the completed triangles as desired.
2. Open the flaps of two touching triangles.

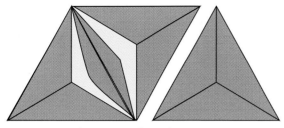

3. Match the fold lines of the flaps with right sides together. Pin across the fold.

4. Sew along the fold line, backstitching at the beginning and at the end.

5. Fold the flaps back to their respective units. Press again to set the seams.

6. Repeat for the number of triangles in a row.

7. Join rows by opening the flaps along the side of the row and matching the fold lines and intersections of the adjoining row. Pin at each intersection.

8. Sew in the fold and backstitch across all the intersections to reinforce the stitching.

Topstitching:

Topstitch ⅝" around the outer edge of the joined units to secure the flaps and stabilize the edge of the project.

Example One: The position of the topstitching in the center joined area will result in several design variations.

1. For the first petal pattern, topstitch from point to point across the middle of the flaps.

2. Turn back the petals between the middle of the joined units and the inner topstitching. Wend the stitching along the edge of the petal by starting in the middle of the joined units. Stitch out to the inner topstitching. Pivot and stitch back from the outer point of the petal.

3. Repeat by pivoting at the inner joined area and stitch the next petal.

4. Once the inner petals are sewn, topstitch the petals in the outer area.

Example Two:

1. Join six complete triangle units, alternating dark and light fabrics for the inner and outer layers.

2. Stitch ½" from the outer edge to secure the loose flaps.

3. Topstitch a 4" diameter circle in the center of the joined units.

5. Form a small flower in the center by turning back the petals between the topstitching and the center of the joined area.

6. Pin the unstitched outer flaps in place at the points.

7. Turn back and topstitch the outermost area of the loose flaps in the petal shapes around the perimeter of the joined units.

8. Turn back and topstitch the remaining areas between the petals to form "bubbles."

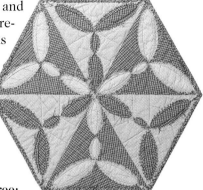

Example Three:
Join six complete triangle units with the dark outside and light inside fabrics.

1. Topstitch ½" from the outer edge.

2. Fold the center of the folded triangle flaps over to ½" from the edge of the unit. Pin.

3. As you fold each flap of the triangle, rotate the unit so the folded areas form a pinwheel effect.

4. Topstitch the folded flaps.

Example Four: Join six complete triangle units with alternating dark and light fabrics.

1. Stitch ½" from the outer edge to secure the loose flaps.

2. Topstitch a 4" diameter circle in the center of the joined units.

3. Form a small flower in the center by turning back the petals between the outer topstitching and the center of the joined area. Topstitch the turned-back petals.

4. Fold the center of each loose flap back upon itself, keeping the point of the flap in the center. Pin in place.

5. Fold the point of the bottom flap so that the point is centered and the fold is horizontal. Pin in place.

6. Repeat the folding and pinning of the remaining triangle units.

7. Topstitch the folded flaps.

8. Turn back and topstitch the loose areas at the outer corners to form small petals.

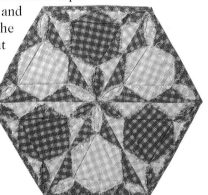

Accented Triangle:

Accents are created by adding a layer of fabric inside the folded unit to form the petal reveal when the flaps are turned back and topstitched. If your inner and outer fabrics are bulky, choose thinner quilting cotton for this layer.

1. With the batting template, cut triangles from the accent fabric.

2. After the joining is complete, layer the triangle on top of the inner fabric of the folded units. Refold the flaps.

3. Turn back and topstitch the flaps.

4. Bind, if desired, with a single layer of bias-cut binding.

Finishing:

1. Apply a scant drop of Fray Check deep into the joined corners on the back and front sides of the centerpiece. Let dry.

2. Toss in the washer and dryer, and fluff.

Twisty-Petal Variations

There are so many variations that you won't want to stop playing! Just six units make this handy centerpiece. With minimal time you can make several for gifts or change your décor anytime! Color placement and petal turn-back variations create many different looks. Add an accent color with a simple third layer.

Finished size: 17" x 19"
Difficulty level: Easy
Block size: 8½" x 9½"

Fabric requirements:
Option One:
⅔ yard light
⅔ yard medium or dark
Option Two:
⅓ yard light
⅓ yard medium
⅓ yard dark
Option Three:
Add ½ yard accent fabric for the petal reveal area.
All Options:
¼ yard 45" wide lightweight batting

Templates:
Triangle template, 2 copies page 88
OR
One purchased plastic hexagon template (see Templates, page 85, for ordering details)

Cutting Plan:
Option One:
6 hexagon cutouts of both fabrics
Option Two:
4 hexagons of each of the 3 fabrics

Option Three:
Add 6 triangles of the accent fabric cut with the batting template

Batting:
6 triangles cut with the batting template

Specific Instructions:
Option One: Layer one hexagon of each fabric. Designate one fabric for the inside and one for the outside. Make all the units alike, or alternate the inner and outer fabrics.
Option Two: Mix and match the inner and outer fabrics.
Option Three: Add the accent triangles after the joining step.

Binding:
Cut and join two 1¼" bias strips. Stitch to the back side with the right sides together. Fold to the front and topstitch along the raw edge.

Finishing:
1. Apply a scant drop of Fray Check deep into the center joined corners on the back and front sides of the quilt. Let dry.
2. Toss the project in the washer and dryer, and fluff.

Heavenly Hexagons 6

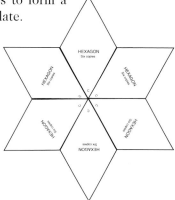

Basic Hexagon

One of the perennial favorites is the hexagon. Lots of petals make pretty flowers, and simple triangles make joining easy. Choose loose-woven fabrics with high-contrast, coordinating, or complementary colors. The projects in this chapter were made from woven and brushed flannel, printed flannel, and homespun. Flannels are substantial enough that batting is optional.

Template Construction:

1. Make six photocopies of the hexagon star template on page 90.
2. Cut along the outer solid line of all six copies.
3. Place three cutout copies on your rotary mat, using the horizontal line of the mat as a guide to align the corners.
4. Tape the diamonds together three at a time. Three pieces make a straight line.
5. Join the halves to form a star-shaped template.

Fabric Selection and Preparation:

In order to accommodate the template, the fabric must measure at least 21 inches square. A project with just two fabrics will have one fabric designated for the inner area that forms the petal reveal. The outer fabric will surround the flowers and form the back side of the project. These two fabrics can be alternated checkerboard style with secondary patterns forming from the illusion. If more than two fabrics are used, separate your selections into inside and outside groups.

Cutting Plan:

All fabric star edges will be cut on the bias to minimize shredding. There are two cutting options.

Option one: You can cut star-shaped pieces from the outer fabric(s) using the paper template. Each of these star-shaped fabric cutouts will be placed on the piece of inner fabric that you have paired with it. The fabric cutout will serve as a template when cutting the inner fabric with scissors. The two layers are perfectly matched and are ready for the folding step.

Option two: For projects with batting, cut all the fabric stars using the paper template, with either scissors or with the rotary ruler and cutter. The batting piece is layered between the outer and inner stars, matching the star points. The star points are then folded to the center to form the hexagons.

For Both Options: Begin by cutting outer fabric stars.

Cutting outer fabric stars:

1. Fold the outside fabric(s) selvedge-to-selvedge, forming two layers.
2. Spray the back side of the paper template with temporary adhesive spray.
3. Place the template on one of the folded fabrics, rotated so that no edge is parallel to the grain line. All edges will be cut on the bias.

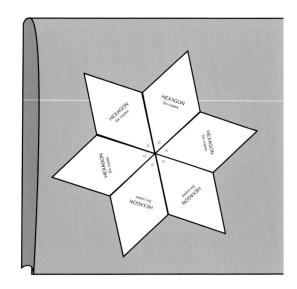

4. Place a rotary ruler on the template, aligning the edge of the ruler with an outer line of the paper template.

5. Cut through both layers of fabric along the edge of the ruler with a rotary cutter. Cut just to the inner corners. (The Olfa® rotary point cutter is handy for precise cutting of the inner corners.) Cutting past the corner will weaken the seams.

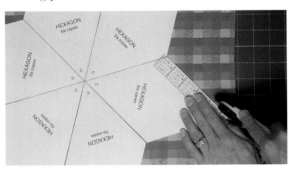

6. Move the ruler around the template, and repeat the cutting until the entire star is cut out. Folded fabric will yield two stars. As an alternative, while being careful to keep the template in place, you can cut the fabric with scissors.

7. Repeat this procedure for the remaining outside fabric(s).

Inner fabric(s)

1. For projects without batting, place an outer star on an inner fabric piece, wrong sides together, rotated so the edges of the star fall on the bias.

2. Using the cutout star as the pattern, cut the

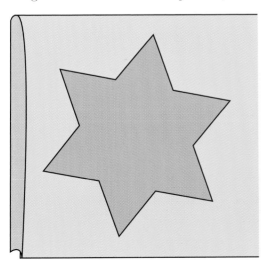

inner fabric layer with a scissors or with a rotary cutter.. Place the rotary ruler so that the edge rests on the cut edge of the first star. Cut along the edge of the ruler. Be careful not to over cut the inner corners.

3. The star cutouts are now perfectly layered and ready to fold. (Remove the extra inner fabric star and match it to another outer star.)

Batting Option:
Thinner fabrics may need a piece of batting inserted between the fabric layers.

1. To prepare a batting template, make two photocopies of the hexagonal-batting template on page 91. Cut along the solid lines of the two copies and join with tape along the center line.

2. Use this template to cut thin lightweight batting (Hobbs Thermore is ideal) with a ruler and rotary cutter into hexagon-shaped pieces. (See the Batting section of Chapter One, page 11.)

3. Place a hexagon-shaped piece of batting centered on the wrong side of the outer fabric star.

4. Layer an inner star on top with the right side up.

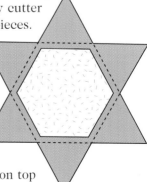

5. Continue with the folding instructions. *Note: There is no need to secure the batting at this point, as it will be sewn to the unit in the top-stitching step below.*

Folding:
Fold the points of the star to the center, forming a hexagon. Press the folds.

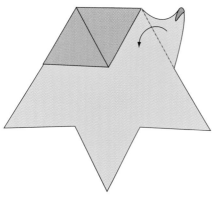

Topstitching:
1. Topstitch ⅝" from the outer edge (over the folds) around all sides of the hexagon.
2. Using topstitching to tack down the center of the unit, sew a circle of stitching that crosses each of the center points. The larger the circle, the greater the amount of "loose" fabric available to form a fuzzy flower center.

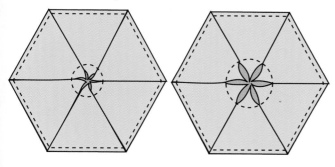

Forming Petals:
1. Turn back the raw edges of the folded flaps between the topstitched areas to form petals. Topstitch along the edge, either with a straight stitch or decorative hemstitch. Placement of the stitching line will determine the degree of fray after laundering. Straight stitching ⅛" from the raw edge will fray less than stitching ¼" away. Hemstitching will decrease the amount of fray by securing more of the raw edges and forming a ridged wavy area outlining the petals.

Laura's hint

Make a test block with several types of topstitching effects, and toss it in the laundry. Choose your preference from the test block.

2. Repeat the topstitching steps for the number of units desired.

Joining:
Hexagons can be joined in two ways: one with patches to fill in the gaps between the units and the other by zigzag stitching over the butted edges of the units. Both have unique features. Patches can form secondary patterns when made from contrasting fabric. They spread the flower blocks out and disperse the pattern. Butting the units concentrates the flower blocks in a smaller area and reduces the number of units to prepare and join. There are fewer steps than with patches, making the process quicker.

Option one: Patch joining method
The completed hexagon units are arranged with the points of the units touching, and the gaps are triangle-shaped. The touching points are joined with bar tack stitching. The open areas are filled and joined with bias-edged triangle patches. These triangles may be matching or contrasting fabric(s). Triangles are layered on the back and front sides of the project with an inner layer of batting to match the thickness of the folded hexagon units.

1. Arrange your hexagon units in the desired pattern.
2. Join two rows of hexagons as a group.
3. Sew the points that form two rows of hexagons with a bar tack (i.e. sewing forward and back several times over the intersection).

4. To prepare a patch triangle template, photocopy the triangle template on page 92.
5. Cut along the solid line.
6. Place the triangle template on the fabric, rotated so that all sides are on the bias.
7. Cut the triangles using a ruler and rotary cutter.

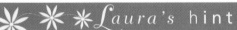

❋ ❋ ❋ *Laura's* hint

Cut the triangles from your star cutting scraps.

8. With the back side of the project facing up, place a bias triangle over each opening in a row by centering the overlapping edges over the open space. The triangle may be sewn or glue basted.

❋ ❋ ❋ *Laura's* hint

It may be easier to lay the joined group on a table and glue baste than to manipulate the group of units through the sewing machine, because the group of joined hexagons is not very stable.

To glue baste: Lift the edge of the triangle and place a small amount of washable fabric glue along the edge of the opening. Center the triangle, and press it on the glued area. Repeat for the row of triangles.

To sew: If you have a fairly large sewing table and wish to sew the back side patch in place, stitch ⅛" from the raw edges. Repeat for the remaining patches.

9. Flip the group of hexagons and triangle patches to the front side.
10. Cut batting triangles using the triangle batting template on page 92.
11. Insert a triangle of batting into the gap between the hexagons. It will sit on top of the back triangle patch.
12. Center the front fabric bias triangle patch over the opening filled with a batting triangle. Pin or glue baste the patch in place. To glue baste, lift an edge of

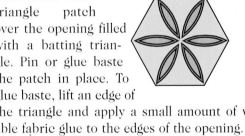

the triangle and apply a small amount of washable fabric glue to the edges of the opening. With your fingers, press the front fabric triangle over the opening so that it's centered.
13. Repeat for the row of hexagons.
14. Sew all the layers of the fabric patches to the hexagons by placing a row of hemstitching along the inner edges of the triangles.

15. Place the layered triangle between the presser foot and the sewing machine. Align the needle with the edge of the hexagon that's between the layers of the bias triangles. Sew along the ridge formed by the folded hexagon so that the stitches catch all the layers of the bias triangle and the edge of the hexagon. The hemstitch zigzag will pierce deeply into the hexagon, securing the triangle to it.

16. Sew inside all three sides of the triangle, keeping the stitching in line with the edge of the folded hexagons.

17. Reverse stitch or tie-off at the end.

18. Repeat for the triangles in the row.

19. Join additional pairs of hexagon rows with the same procedure.

20. Combine the joined rows in pairs until all rows are joined.

Add edge pieces:
1. Cut bias-edged triangles with the triangle template (page 92). Fold the edge triangles in half vertically.
2. On the back side of the project, baste one half of the triangle to the opening along the edge of the project by lifting the edge of the triangle and applying a small amount of glue along the edge of the opening.
3. Continue glue basting triangles along one edge.
4. Cut batting triangles using the template on page 92. Cut these triangles in half vertically.
5. Flip the project to the right side, and insert these triangles of batting into the openings along the side of the project.
6. Fold the triangle to the front, over the batting triangle.
7. Lift the edge of a triangle, and apply a small amount of fabric glue along the edge of the opening. With your fingers, press the folded triangle on the glue.
8. Repeat for the remaining triangles along this side.

9. Sew the layered triangles to the folded hexagons with zigzag or hemstitching as in step 16 of the previous section.
10. Repeat the application of folded triangles along the remaining three sides of the project.

Option Two: Joining without patches
1. Arrange the completed hexagon units in the desired pattern so that the units touch each other along the fold lines without any gaps.
2. Stitch the units together with zigzag topstitching along the joints.

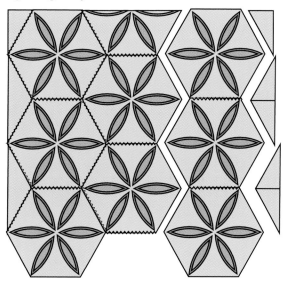

3. Fill in the top and bottom gaps by cutting whole units in half horizontally. The edges along the sides can be filled in with units that have been cut in thirds.
4. After all the units are joined, apply a scant drop of Fray Check deep into the joined corners. Let dry.

Binding:
Refer to the Binding Section in Chapter One, page 17.

Finishing:
1. Toss the project in the washer and dryer. Check the lint trap, and clean it often during drying.
2. Fluff the flower petals.

Petals in Pink

Finished size: 40" x 52"
Difficulty level: Intermediate
Block size: 8" x 10"

Fabric requirements:
Marcus Brothers flannels
    4 yards pink floral
    3½ yards pink plaid
    7 yards solid pink brushed
    ½ yard solid green brushed
¾ yard 45" wide lightweight batting

Binding:
Included in the solid pink fabric

Templates:
Hexagon star template, 6 copies page 90
Triangle patch template, 1 copy page 92
Batting triangle template, 1 copy page 92

Cutting Plan:
24 solid pink flannel hexagons
12 pink floral hexagons
12 pink plaid hexagons
4 pink floral 4½" strips cut into 48 triangles
4 solid green 4½" strips cut into 48 triangles
6 solid pink 1½" wide bias binding strips
48 batting strips, 4" wide, cut into triangles

Specific Instructions:
1. Cut three finished hexagons in half vertically for edge pieces.
2. Insert the halves along the sides as shown in the photo.
3. Refer to Joining, option one, on page 58.
4. Use the green triangle patches on the back side to form star shapes.
5. Stitch across the triangle patches to secure the batting.

Binding:
1. Join the binding strips. Stitch to the back side of the project with right sides together.
2. Fold the binding to the front, and stitch ¼" from the folded edge, leaving the folded edge raw.

Drown yourself in pink flowers. This feminine quilt is perfect for a little girl's room.

The back side is just as pretty as the front, with sweet stars formed by green patch triangles.

Finishing:
1. Apply a scant drop of Fray Check deep into the center joined corners on the back and front sides of the quilt. Let dry.
2. Toss the quilt into the washer and dryer.
3. Check the lint filter often during the drying cycle.
4. Fluff.

Fuzzy Flowers

Fuzzy flowers bloom all over this colorful quilt.

Finished size: 60" x 64"
Difficulty level: Intermediate
Block size: 9" x 10"

Fabric requirements:
AE Nathan flannel*
  8 yards blue green plaid
  3 yards blue check
  3 yards green check
  3 yards gold check
*Yardage is based on 60" wide fabric.

Binding:
Included in the blue check fabric

Templates:
Hexagon star template, 6 copies page 90
OR
Purchased plastic hexagon star template (see templates, page 85, for ordering details)
Diamond filler template, 2 copies page 96

Cutting Plan:
47 blue-green plaid hexagons
15 blue hexagons
16 green hexagons
16 gold hexagons
9 blue-green plaid corner diamonds
4 green diamonds
4 blue check diamonds
1 gold diamond
6 blue check 1⅛" wide bias binding strips

Edge and corner pieces:

1. Cut two of the hexagons in half.
2. Insert the halves along the top and bottom, as shown in the photo.

3. Prepare edge pieces using the diamond instructions, page 44.

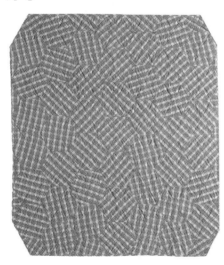

4. Cut two green, two blue, and one gold diamond in half vertically for the side filler pieces.
5. Join the units into rows with overedge zigzag stitches. Join the rows with zigzag topstitching across the butted hexagon rows.

Binding:

1. Join the binding strips. Stitch to the back side of the project with right sides together.
2. Fold the binding to the front and stitch ¼" from the folded edge, leaving the folded edge raw.

Finishing:

1. Apply a scant drop of Fray Check deep into the center joined corners on the back and front sides of the quilt. Let dry.
2. Toss the quilt into the washer and dryer.
3. Check the lint trap often during the drying cycle.
4. Fluff.

Accented hexagon

Add a third color to the hexagons by inserting a fabric cutout under the folded flaps. This fabric will be the revealed area in the petals. It can be made from coordinating flannels, home spun, or even quilt cottons. The insert's edges will be sealed inside the unit.

1. Place the hexagon batting template on the accent fabric. Cut along the edge of the template with a ruler and rotary cutter.
2. Repeat for the remaining inserts.
3. Insert the accent fabric hexagon under the folded flaps of the hexagon before the topstitching step.
4. Continue with the folding, topstitching, and petal-turning steps.

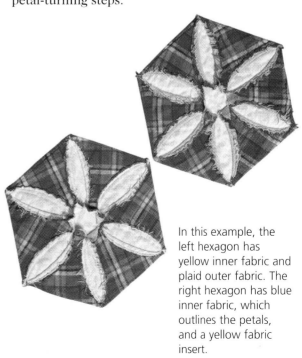

In this example, the left hexagon has yellow inner fabric and plaid outer fabric. The right hexagon has blue inner fabric, which outlines the petals, and a yellow fabric insert.

7 Oscillating Octagons

Basic Octagon

One of my favorites is the octagon because there are lots of petals in the flowers and simple squares make joining easy. One characteristic of octagons is that they fray more evenly and have fewer stringy pieces than hexagons. They can be mixed and matched with squares and rectangles too. Choose loose-woven fabrics with high-contrast, coordinating, or complementary colors. The projects in this chapter were made from a woven and brushed flannel, printed flannel, and homespun. Most flannels are substantial enough that batting is optional.

Template Construction:
1. Make eight photocopies of the octagon template on page 94.
2. Cut along the outer solid line of all eight copies.
3. Place two diamond-shaped cutouts on your rotary mat at right angles, using the crossed lines of the mat as guides.
4. Matching the corners, tape the diamonds together two at a time. Four pieces make a straight line.
5. Join the halves to form a star-shaped template.

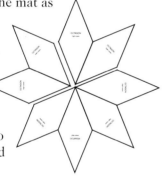

Fabric Selection and Preparation:
In order to accommodate the template, fabric pieces must measure at least 21 inches square.
A project with just two fabrics will have one fabric designated for the inner area that forms the petal reveal. The outer fabric will surround the flowers and form the back side of the project. If more than two fabrics are used, separate your selections into inside and outside groups.

Cutting Plan:
All fabric-star edges will be cut on the bias to minimize shredding.
Option One: You can cut star-shaped pieces from the outer fabric(s) using the paper template. Each of these star-shaped fabric cutouts will be placed on the piece of inner fabric that you have paired with it. The fabric cutout will serve as a template

when cutting the inner fabric with scissors. The two layers are perfectly matched and are ready for the folding step.
Option Two: For projects with batting, cut all the fabric stars using the paper template with either scissors or with the rotary ruler and cutter. The batting piece is layered between the outer and inner stars, matching the star points. The star points are then folded to form the octagons.
For Both Options: Begin by cutting outer fabric stars.

Cutting Outer Fabric Stars:
1. Fold the outside fabric(s) selvedge-to-selvedge, forming two layers.
2. Spray the back side of the paper template with temporary adhesive spray.
3. Place the template on one of the folded fabrics, rotated so that no edge is parallel to the grain line. All edges will be cut on the bias.

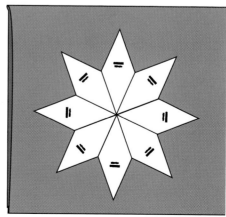

4. Place a rotary ruler on the template, lining up the edge of the ruler with an outer line of the paper template.

5. Cut through both layers of fabric along the edge of the ruler with a rotary cutter just to the inner corners. (Olfa's rotary point cutter is handy for precise cutting of the inner corners.) Cutting past the corner will weaken the seams.

6. Move the ruler around the template, and repeat the cutting until the entire star is cut out. Folded fabric will yield two stars. As an alternative, while being careful to keep the template in place, you can cut the fabric with scissors.

7. Repeat this procedure for the remaining outside fabric(s).

Inner Fabric(s):

1. For projects without batting, place an outer star on an inner fabric piece, wrong sides together, rotated so the edges of the star fall on the bias.

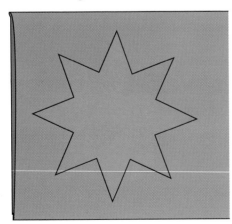

2. Using the cutout star as the pattern, cut the inner fabric layer with scissors or a rotary cutter and ruler. The cutout stars are now perfectly layered and ready to fold. (Remove the extra inner fabric star and match it to another outer star.)

Batting:

For thinner fabric, insert a batting cutout between the inner and outer fabric layers.

1. Prepare a batting template by making two copies of the octagonal batting template on page 93. Cut the two copies along the solid lines and join with tape along the centerline.

2. Use this template to cut thin lightweight batting (Hobbs Thermore is ideal) with a ruler and rotary cutter. (See the Batting section in Chapter One, page 11.)

3. Center an octagon-shaped piece of batting on the wrong side of the outer fabric star. *Note: There is no need to secure the batting at this point, as it will be sewn to the unit in the top-stitching step.*

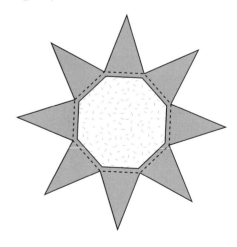

4. Layer an inner star on top with the right side up.

Folding:

1. Fold the points of the star to the center, forming an octagon.
2. Press.

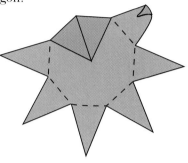

Topstitching:

1. Topstitch approximately ½" from the outer edge (over the folds) around all sides of the octagon.
2. Using topstitching to tack down the center of the unit, sew a circle of stitching that crosses each of the center points. The larger the circle, the greater the amount of "loose" fabric that's available to form a fuzzy flower center.

The octagon in the corner has a larger center area than the octagons with gold petals adjacent to it.

Forming Petals:

1. Turn back the raw edges of the folded flaps - between the topstitched areas to form petals. Topstitch along the edge either with a straight stitch or hemstitch. Placement of the stitching line will determine the degree of fray after laundering. Straight stitching ⅛" from the raw edge makes more fray than stitching ¼" away. Hemstitching will decrease the amount of fray by securing more of the raw edges and forming a ridged wavy area outlining the petals.

Laura's hint

Make a sample block with several types of topstitching effects and toss it in the laundry. Choose your preference from the test block.

2. Repeat the topstitching steps for the number of units desired.

Joining:

The four common sides of the octagons that meet are joined with zigzag stitching. The open areas are filled and joined with bias square patches. These squares may be cut from matching or contrasting fabric(s). Squares are layered on the back and front sides of the project with an inner layer of batting to match the thickness of the folded octagon units.

1. Arrange your octagon units in the desired pattern. Joining two rows of octagons as a group is easier to manage than joining the whole project at once.
2. Sew the common sides of two rows of octagons together with a zigzag topstitch. Use fancy or contrasting thread for an additional design, or hide the stitches with matching thread.

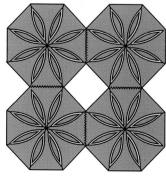

Patches:

The patches that are layered to fill the gaps between the primary octagon units are squares, half-square triangles, and quarter-square triangles.

1. Use the templates on page 93 to cut the half- and quarter-square triangles for the back and front of the project. (It's logical to cut squares in half and half again; but, one or more of the edges will be on grain. The on-grain edges will shred and degrade. Therefore, cut the triangles with the templates to assure bias edges.)

2. For the square openings, cut 4¾" bias-cut squares for the front and back side of your project. They may be matching, contrasting, or coordinating fabrics.

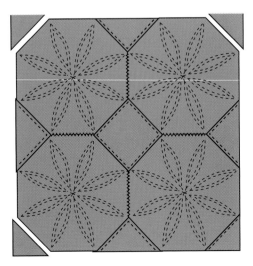

✳ ❋ ✳ *Laura's hint*

Cut the patches from your star-cutting scraps.

3. With the back side of the project facing up, place a bias-cut patch over each opening in a row by centering the overlapping edges over the open space.

4. Sew or glue-baste the patches to the back side of the project.

To sew: Stitch ⅛" from the raw edge around all sides of the patch. Repeat for the remaining patches.

To glue-baste: Lift the edge of the patch, and place a small amount of washable fabric glue along the edge of the opening.

Center the patch, and press it onto the glued area. Repeat for the remaining patches in the row.

5. Flip the group of octagons and patches to the front side.

Batting inserts:

Batting inserts are squares, half-square triangles, and quarter-square triangles that are inserted in the gap between the octagons to match the thickness of the primary units.

1. Prepare the inserts by cutting 4" squares of batting. Divide the squares in half, and then in half again to make the necessary number of half- and quarter-square triangles of batting for the project.

2. Insert batting squares and triangles into the gaps between the octagons.

3. Place front fabric patches over the batting inserts, centering the edges over the gaps. Pin the patches in place or glue-baste by applying a small amount of washable fabric glue to the edges of the opening and pressing the patch on the glue.

4. Repeat for the row of octagons.
5. Sew the fabric patches by placing a row of hemstitching along the edges of the octagons.
6. Place the layered patch between the presser foot and the sewing machine. Line up the needle with the ridge formed by the folded sides of the octagon inside the layers of the patch. Sew along the ridge of the folded octagon so that the stitches catch all the layers of the bias square and the edge of the octagon. The hemstitch zigzag will swing over into the octagon, securing the patch to it.

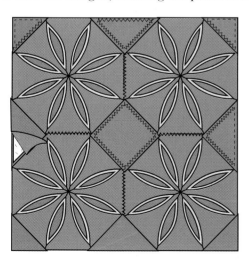

7. Sew inside the patch sides, keeping the stitching in line with the edge of the folded octagons. Reverse stitch or tie-off at the end.
8. Repeat for the remaining patches.
9. Join additional pairs of octagon rows with the same procedure.
10. Combine the joined rows in pairs until all rows are joined.
11. Add edge pieces with the same procedure. Secure the outer raw edges with straight stitching through the patch layers and the batting.
12. Topstitch across the patches to secure the batting.

Binding:
1. Refer to the Bind and Finish section, page 17.
2. Bind with a single layer of bias binding.

Finishing:
1. Toss the bound project in the washer and dryer.
2. Check the lint trap often during the drying cycle, and fluff when dry.

Mixed Greens

Here's a chance to mix up some greens! Sparkling octagon flowers are bordered by fences of rectangles and squares. This quilt makes a pretty table cover or warm wrap on a chilly day. Show it off as a sofa throw. Bring summer inside all year!

Finished size: 45" x 60"
Difficulty level: Easy
Block size: Octagon 10" x 10", Rectangle 5" x 10", Square 5"

Fabric requirements:
Marcus Brother's flannel
  8 yards purple floral
  2 yards light gold
  2 yards medium gold
  3½ yards butter cream

Binding:
Included in the purple floral fabric

Templates:
Octagon template, 8 copies page 94
OR
Purchased plastic octagon star template (see templates, page 85, for ordering details)
Rectangle template—2 sheets of paper, 8½" x 11"
Patch template, 1 copy page 93

Cutting Plan:
20 floral octagons
8 light gold octagons
8 medium gold octagons
4 butter cream octagons
13 floral rectangles
13 butter cream rectangles
2 floral 7⅛" bias-cut squares
2 butter cream 7⅛" bias-cut squares
3 floral 1⅛" wide bias binding strips

Floral Patches (cut from scraps):
4 front and 4 back 4¾" bias squares
8 front and 8 back 4¾" bias squares
12 front and 12 back bias half-square triangles
20 front and 20 back bias quarter-square triangles

Layout:
Refer to the photograph for layout.

Specific Instructions:
The rectangle units are sized to match the octagon units. Complete the rectangle, square, and octagon units through the petal topstitching step.

1. **Rectangles.** To make the rectangle template, cut two 5" x 10" rectangles from two pieces of paper. Draw a diagonal line from one top corner to the opposite bottom corner on both sheets. Cut along the line. Refer to Template Construction, page 37, to assemble the template.

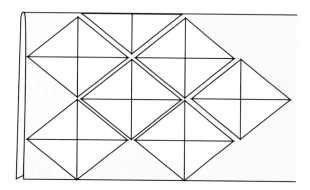

2. Using this cutting diagram as a guide, cut 13 rectangles from both the floral and the butter cream flannels. Layer, fold, and topstitch (see pages 38-39).

3. **Patches.** All sides of the patch shapes need to be cut on the bias. For the half and quarter square triangles, cut the pieces using the templates on page 93. These pieces may be cut from the star scrap fabric.

4. **Squares.** Cut two 7⅛" bias squares from the floral fabric and the butter cream flannel. Layer, fold, and topstitch (see pages 20-21).

Assembly:
Join with zigzag stitching and patches (see pages 67-69).

Binding:
Join the binding strips. Stitch the binding with right sides together to the back side of the quilt. Fold the raw edge of the binding to the front, and stitch ¼" from the folded edge.

Finishing:
1. Toss the bound project in the washer and dryer.
2. Check the lint trap often during the drying cycle, and fluff when dry.

*B*right *Blossoms (cover quilt)*

Bright and bold colors burst from these striking flowers.

Finished size: 58" x 70"
Difficulty level: Intermediate
Block size: 10" square

Fabric requirements:
AE Nathan brushed flannels*
   8 yards purple plaid
   3 yards purple check
   3⅓ yards gold check
   2¼ yards red check
⅔ yard 45" wide lightweight batting
* Yardage is based on 58" to 60" wide fabric.

Binding:
Included in the purple plaid fabric

Templates:
Octagon template, 8 copies page 94
OR

Purchased plastic octagon star template (see templates, page 85, for ordering details)
Octagon batting and patch templates, 2 copies page 93

Cutting Plan:
42 purple plaid octagon stars
14 purple check octagon stars
16 gold check octagon stars
12 red check octagon stars
52 purple-plaid 4¾" bias-cut square patches cut from the scraps of the cut stars
30 mixed fabric 4¾" bias-cut squares from the 3 check fabrics for the back
7 purple plaid 1¼" wide bias binding strips or 5 purple plaid 2" wide folded straight grain binding strips
30 squares of thin batting, 4" x 4"
11 squares of thin batting cut diagonally into 22 triangles

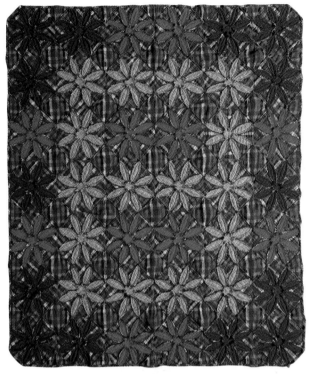

Specific Instructions:

1. Insert bias square patches between the joined octagons.
2. Fold 22 plaid bias squares diagonally.
3. Insert a triangle of batting between the layers.
4. Stitch these patches in the gaps, along the outer edge, using a zigzag hemstitch.
5. Topstitch through the square and triangle patches to secure the batting.

Binding:

1. Join the binding strips.
2. Stitch to the back side with the right sides together. Fold the binding to the front, and stitch ¼" from the folded edge.

Finishing:

1. Toss the bound project in the washer and dryer.
2. Check the lint trap often during the drying cycle, and fluff when dry.

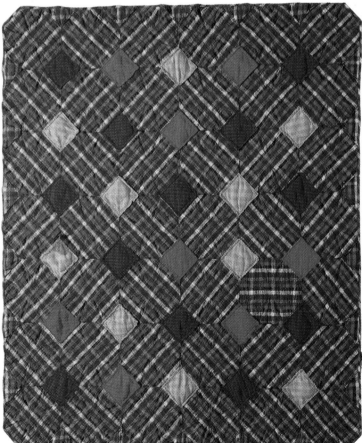

Note the one octagon that's rotated in this photo of the back side.

Black and White and Red All Over

Bright and bold colors burst with a fireworks effect.

Finished size: 28" square
Difficulty level: Intermediate
Block size: 9½" Octagon, 4½" Square

Fabric requirements:
3 yards black plaid homespun
3 yards white osnaburg
1 yard red print quilt cotton
⅛ yard 45" wide lightweight batting

Templates:
Octagon template, 2 copies page 94
OR
Purchased plastic octagon star template (see Templates, page 85, for ordering detail)
Octagon batting and patch templates, 2 copies page 93
Small triangle template (use the dodecagon batting triangle), 1 copy page 95

Cutting Plan:
9 black plaid octagons
9 white octagons
9 red plaid octagon inserts
8 black bias square patches, 4¾" x 4¾"
4 red 3" bias squares for accents
4 white 2" triangles for accents
5 black 1¼" wide bias strips or 5 black 2" wide folded straight grain strips
4 squares of thin batting, 4"
4 squares of thin batting cut diagonally into 8 triangles

Specific Instructions:

1. To make accents, layer a white triangle on each of the red three-inch bias-cut squares. Stitch ¼" from the edge on all four sides.
2. Repeat for the remaining red squares.
3. Add these accent patches after all the joining is complete. Layer a red square on each of the black plaid patches.
4. Stitch ¼" from the raw edges.
5. Repeat for the remaining accents.

Binding:
Join the binding strips, and stitch with the raw edge folded to the front.

Finishing:
1. Toss the bound project in the washer and dryer.
2. Check the lint trap often during the drying cycle, and fluff when dry.

Doodling Dodecagons 7

*B*asic *D*odecagon

Sunflowers and daisies bloom over these bright and cheery quilts! Maximize texture with abundant multi-petaled flowers. Choose springy pastels, bright summery yellows, or rich deep purples. Construction is just as easy as the other flower patterns. Choose coordinating inner and outer fabrics and an optional accent. Mix and match for a diverse bouquet.

Template Construction:

The template can be made half the size and placed on the fold.*

1. Make six photocopies of the dodecagon template on page 94. Cut along the outer solid line of all six copies.

2. Cut one of the diamonds in half in the long direction, and piece the two halves as shown in the photo.

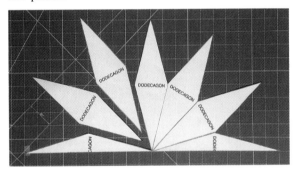

3. By creating the template with this offset, the fabric edges are cut on the bias.

* Or, cut 12 copies and join them to make the whole star template.

Fabric Selection and Preparation:

In order to accommodate the template, fabric pieces must measure at least 21 inches square. A project with just two fabrics will have one fabric designated for the inner area that forms the petal reveal. The outer fabric will surround the flowers and form the back side of the project. If more than two fabrics are used, separate your selections into inside and outside groups.

Cutting Plan:

All fabric star edges will be cut on the bias to minimize shredding. Dodecagon stars are cut using the half size template placed on folded fabric. There are two cutting options. Specific instructions follow the introduction.

Option One: Cut star-shaped pieces from the outer fabric(s) with the paper template. Each of these star-shaped fabric cutouts will be placed on the piece of inner fabric that you have paired with it. The fabric cutout will serve as a template when cutting the inner fabric with scissors. The two layers are perfectly matched and ready for the folding step. There is no batting layer in this option.

Option Two: For projects with batting, cut all the fabric stars using the paper template with either scissors or with the rotary ruler and cutter. The batting piece is layered between the outer and inner stars, matching the star points. The star points are then folded to form the dodecagons.

For Both Options: Begin by cutting outer fabric stars.

Cutting outer fabric stars:

1. With right sides out, fold each selvedge of the outside fabric(s) to the fold line in the center.

2. Spray the back side of the paper template with temporary adhesive spray.

3. Place the template on one folded edge of the fabric so that the straight edge of the template is on the fold.

4. Place a rotary ruler on the template, lining up the edge of the ruler with an outer line of the paper template.

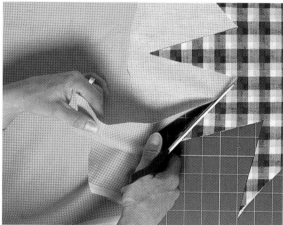

5. Cut through both layers of fabric along the edge of the ruler with a rotary cutter just to the inner corners. (Olfa's rotary point cutter is handy for precise cutting of the inner corners.) Cutting past the corner will weaken the seams.

6. Move the ruler around the template and repeat the cutting until the entire star is cut out. As an alternative, while being careful to keep the template in place, you can cut the fabric with scissors.

7. Unfold the fabric star, and press the fold lines flat.

8. Repeat this procedure for the remaining outside fabric(s).

Inner fabric(s):

If you are working with long yardage, you may wish to cut the inner fabrics into 21-inch lengths.

1. For projects without batting, place an outer star on an inner fabric piece, wrong sides together, rotated so the edges of the star fall on the bias.

✽ ✽ ✽ Laura's hint

If your fabric is striped or plaid, use the lines of the fabric to make sure your star edges are on the bias.

2. Using the cutout star as the pattern, cut the inner fabric layer with a scissors or with a rotary cutter and ruler.

3. The cut-out stars are now perfectly layered and ready to fold. (Remove the extra inner star and match it to another outer star.)

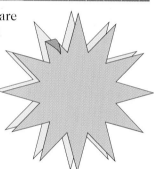

Inserting Optional Batting Cutouts:

1. Prepare a batting template by making two photocopies of the dodecagon batting template on page 95.

2. Cut the two copies along the solid lines, and join them with tape along the center line. Use this template to cut thin lightweight batting (Hobbs Thermore is ideal) with a ruler and rotary cutter into dodecagon-shaped pieces. (See the Batting section in Chapter One, page 11.)

3. Place a dodecagon-shaped piece of batting centered inside the fold lines on the wrong side of the outer fabric star. ***Note: There is no need to secure the batting at this point, as it will be sewn to the unit in the topstitching step on the next page.***

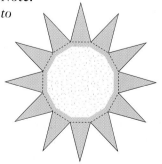

4. Layer an inner star on top with the right side up.

Folding:
1. Fold the points of the star to the center, forming a dodecagon.

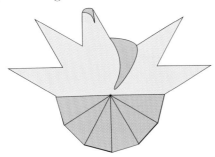

2. Press.

Accent color option:
Create unique accents by adding a third color for the petal reveal and flower center areas. This accent fabric can be made from decorative, novelty, or quilting cotton fabric.

1. Cut a fabric insert using the batting template.
2. Place the batting template on the petal-reveal fabric, and cut it with the rotary cutter and ruler.
3. Place the cut piece centered on the inner fabric star. Refold the flaps to the center.

4. Topstitch ⅜" from the outer edge to seal the insert within the stitching.
5. Continue with Topstitching step #2 (below) to secure the center flaps.

Topstitching:
1. Topstitch approximately ½" from the outer edge (over the folds) around all sides of the dodecagon.
2. Using topstitching to tack down the center of the unit, sew a circle of stitching that crosses each of the center points.

3. The larger the circle, the more "loose" fabric will be available to form the fuzzy flower center.

Forming Petals:
1. To form petal shapes, turn back the loose bias edges of the folded flaps (i.e. the area between the center and outer topstitching). Set your sewing machine to your desired stitch type. Placement of the stitching line will determine the degree of fray after laundering. Straight stitching ⅛" from the raw edge reduces fraying more than stitching ¼" away. Decorative hemstitching and zigzag variations will decrease the amount of fray by securing more of the raw edges.

✿ ✲ ✳ ʟaura's hint

Make a test block with several types of topstitching effects, and toss it in the laundry. Choose your preference from the test block.

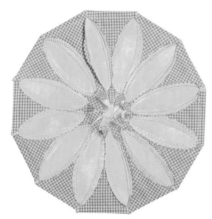

2. Repeat the topstitching steps for the number of units desired.

Joining:

The three common sides of the dodecagons that meet are joined with zigzag stitching. The open areas in between are filled and joined with bias triangle patches. These triangles may be of matching or contrasting fabric(s). Triangles are layered on the back and front sides of the project with an inner layer of batting to match the thickness of the folded dodecagon units.

1. Arrange your dodecagon units in the desired pattern. Joining two rows of dodecagons as a group is easier to manage than joining the whole project at once.

2. Sew the common sides of two rows of dodecagons together with a zigzag topstitch. Use fancy or contrasting thread for an additional design, or hide the stitches with matching thread.

3. Repeat for the remaining units in the row.

Patch Triangles:

Using the triangle batting template, cut bias-edged triangles for the front and back sides of your project. They may be matching, contrasting, or coordinating fabrics.

Laura's hint

Cut the triangles from your star-cutting scraps.

1. Photocopy the triangle template on page 92. Cut along the solid line.

2. Place the template on the fabric, rotated so that all edges are on the bias. Cut with a ruler and rotary cutter along the sides of the template.

3. Repeat for the number of triangles needed for the front and back side of the project.

4. With the back side of the project facing up, place a bias triangle over each opening in a row by centering the overlapping edges over the open space. Sew ⅛" from the raw edge on all three sides. An alternative would be to lift the edge of the triangle and glue-baste by placing a small amount of washable fabric glue along the edge of the opening.

Center the triangle, and press it on the glued area.

5. Repeat for the row of triangles.

6. Flip the group of dodecagons and triangle patches to the front side.

7. Cut batting triangles using the batting template on page 95.

8. Insert a triangle of batting into the gap between the dodecagons, on top of the back triangle fabric patch.

9. Center the bias front fabric triangle patch over the opening.

10. Pin or glue baste the patch in place. To glue baste, lift the edges of the triangle and apply a small amount of washable fabric glue to the edges of the opening. Replace the triangle, and press with your fingers to secure it in position.

11. Repeat for the row of dodecagons.

12. Hemstitch the edges of the triangles by placing the layered triangle between the presser foot and the sewing machine. Line up the needle with the edge of the dodecagon that's inside the layers of the bias triangles. Sew along the ridge of the folded dodecagon so that the stitches catch all the layers of the bias triangle and the edge of the dodecagon. The hemstitch zigzag will pierce deeply into the dodecagon, securing the triangle to it.

13. Sew inside all sides of the triangle, keeping the stitching in line with the edge of the folded dodecagons. Reverse stitch or tie-off at the end.

14. Repeat for the triangles in the row.

15. Join additional pairs of dodecagon rows with the same procedure.

16. Combine the joined rows in pairs until all rows are joined.

Edge pieces:

1. Fill in the notched edge areas with patch triangles. Finish the raw outer edges by hemstitching ¼" from the edge. This area will be encased in binding.

2. Sew layered triangles to the folded dodecagons as in step 13 above.

3. Repeat along the remaining sides of the project.

4. Add accent circles to flower centers if desired.

Binding:
Refer to the Binding Section in Chapter One, page 17.

Sunny Squiggles

Finished size: 45" x 50"
Difficulty level: Advanced
Block size: 10" x 10"

Fabric requirements:
Westfalenstoffe homespun*
   2½ yards orange check
   1⅔ yards light green check
   2 yards yellow check
   2½ yards green plaid
½ yard 45" wide light-
   weight batting
* Yardage is based on 58"
to 60" wide fabric.

Binding:
½ yard light green check

Templates:
Dodecagon template, 6 copies page
   94
OR
Purchased plastic template (see
   Templates, page 85, for ordering
   details)
Dodecagon triangle patch template, 1
   copy page 95
Dodecagon triangle patch batting tem-
   plate, 1 copy page 95

Cutting Plan:
10 orange inner dodecagons
7 light green check outer dodecagons
9 yellow check inner dodecagons
12 green plaid outer dodecagons
72 light green check patch triangles
5 light green check 2" wide
   bias binding strips
36 triangle batting patches

Specific Instructions:
After topstitching and turning
back the petals, arrange the flowers with the light outer fabric in the
inner circle and the dark around the
outside.

Brighten up your kitchen with a splash of
sunflowers. This bright table cover will liven up
any space. Hang it on the wall for a focal point to
your décor. Single flower units can be used for
mats. Hemstitch fabric squares for matching
napkins.

Binding:
Bind with the five 2" wide
   bias-cut light green check
   binding strips. Fold the
   joined strips in half.
   Wrap the strip around
   the outer edge. Stitch
   through the layers.

Finishing:
Toss the quilt into the
washer and dryer, and fluff.

Dancing Daisies

Spring has sprung in a glorious bouquet of pastel daisies. Wrap yourself in this cuddly blanket on a cool summer's eve. Make one for a special friend.

Finished size: 60" x 62"
Difficulty level: Intermediate
Block size: 10" x 10"

Fabric requirements:
AE Nathan flannels*
   8 yards pink plaid brushed flannel
   3 yards yellow check flannel
   3 yards blue check flannel
   3 yards green check flannel

3 yards 45" wide lightweight batting
* Yardage is based on 58" to 60" wide fabric.

Binding:
Included in the pink plaid

Templates:
Dodecagon star template, 6 copies page 94
OR
Purchased plastic template (see Templates, page

85, for ordering information

Dodecagon batting template, 2 copies page 95

Dodecagon triangle patch template, 1 copy page 95

Dodecagon triangle patch batting template, 1 copy page 95

Cutting Plan:

36 pink plaid dodecagon stars

14 yellow check dodecagon stars

11 blue check dodecagon stars

11 green check dodecagon stars

72 pink plaid front triangle patches

72 mixed checks back triangle patches

6 pink plaid 1¼" wide bias binding strips

36 dodecagon batting inserts

72 triangle batting patches

Specific Instructions:

1. Layer batting between the inner and outer pieces.

2. Arrange the daisies in rows with the inner flower colors mixed. Cut four dodecagons in half for the edge pieces.

3. Topstitch through the triangle patches to secure the batting.

Layout:

Refer to the photo.

Binding:

Bind with the six joined pink plaid 1¼" wide bias binding strips. Fold the joined strips in half. Wrap the folded strip around the outer edge. Stitch through all layers.

Finishing:

Toss the quilt into the washer and dryer, and fluff.

Back side of the quilt.

A final word

I hope you've had lots of fun making raggedy, fuzzy, curly, and twisty quilts! Share the fun with your friends and family. Bring joy to their lives with a cozy comforting wrap. Play with fabric, color, and texture. Explore new ideas. Teach someone to sew these easy projects.

Look for more projects with exciting new designs and fabric combinations. There will be mixing and matching of shapes, embellishments, and wearables! I'm looking forward to sharing them with you.

Sit back, relax, breathe, and dream...

Templates

For questions, additional information, rigid plastic templates, and products, consult my Web site: www.fastfoldedflowers.com or email: laurafarson@fastfoldedflowers.com

fold line

STARRY SQUARE
TWO COPIES

grain line

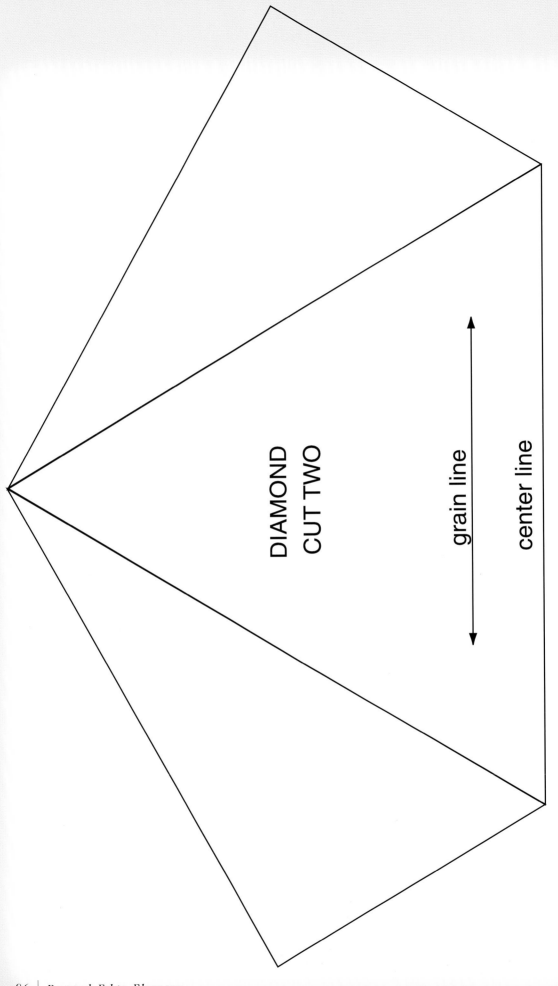

DIAMOND
CUT TWO

grain line

center line

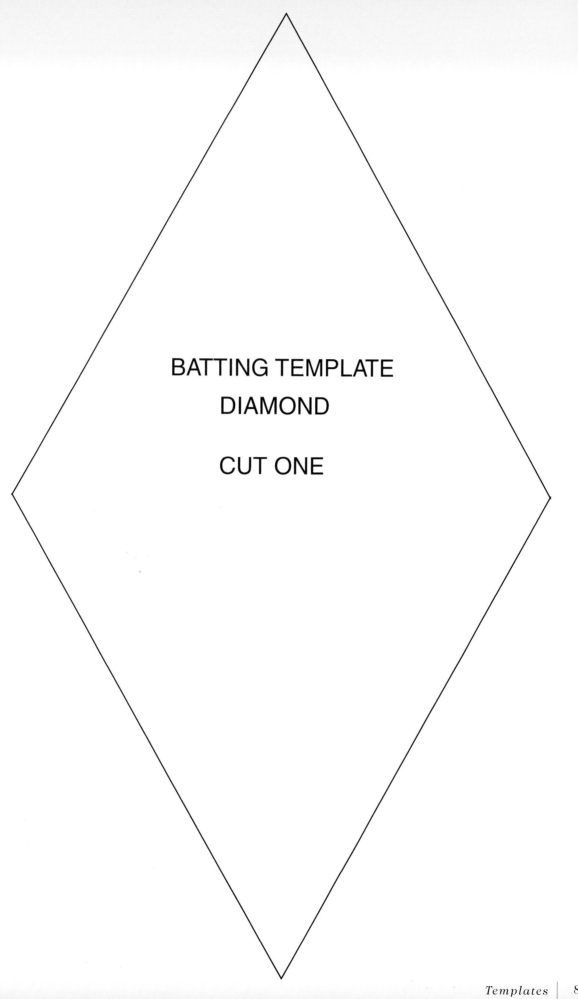

BATTING TEMPLATE
DIAMOND

CUT ONE

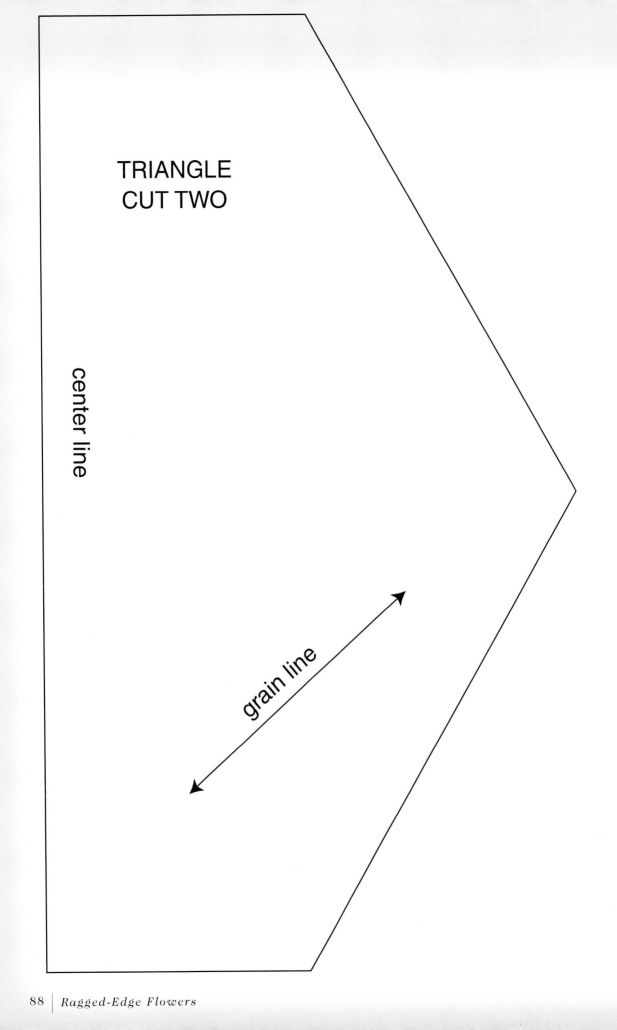

TRIANGLE
CUT TWO

center line

grain line

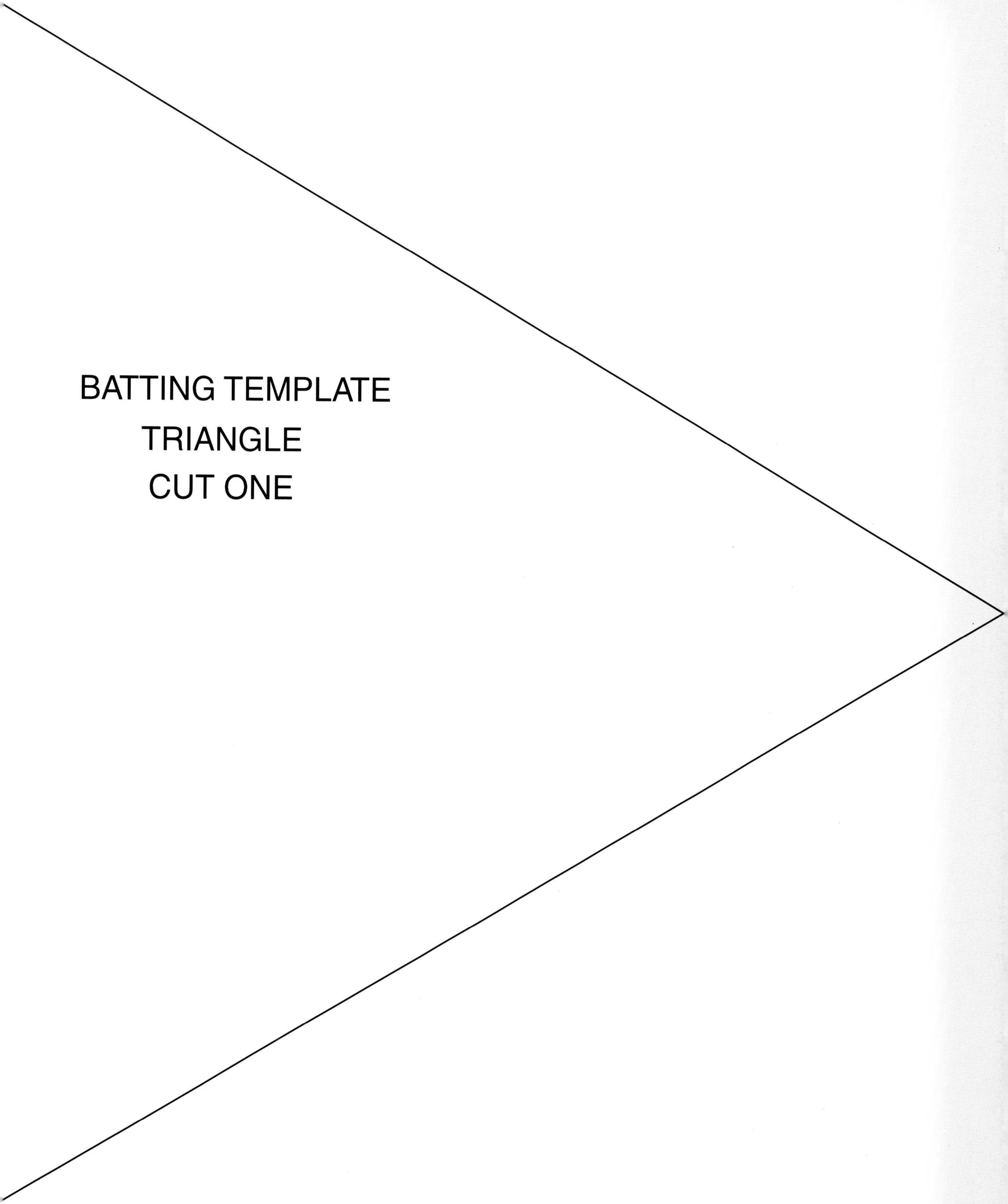

BATTING TEMPLATE
TRIANGLE
CUT ONE

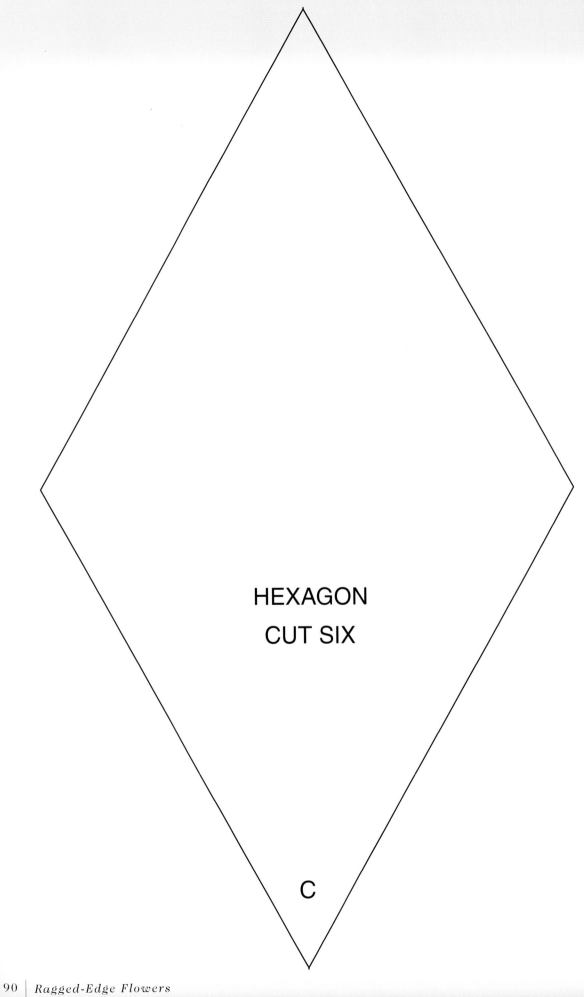

HEXAGON

CUT SIX

C

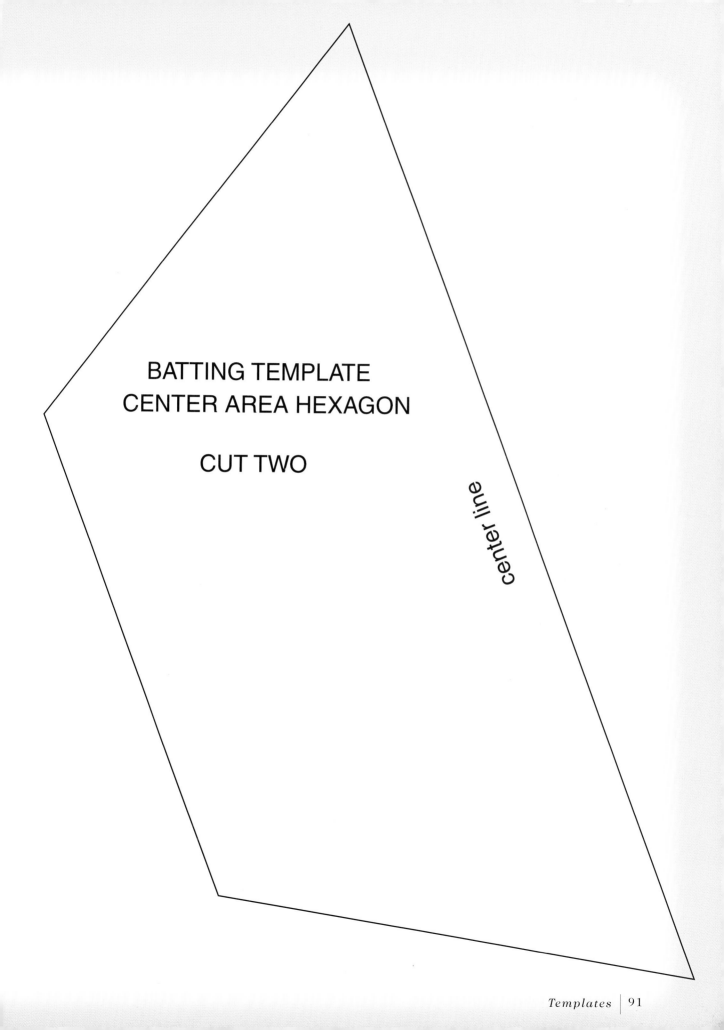

BATTING TEMPLATE
CENTER AREA HEXAGON

CUT TWO

center line

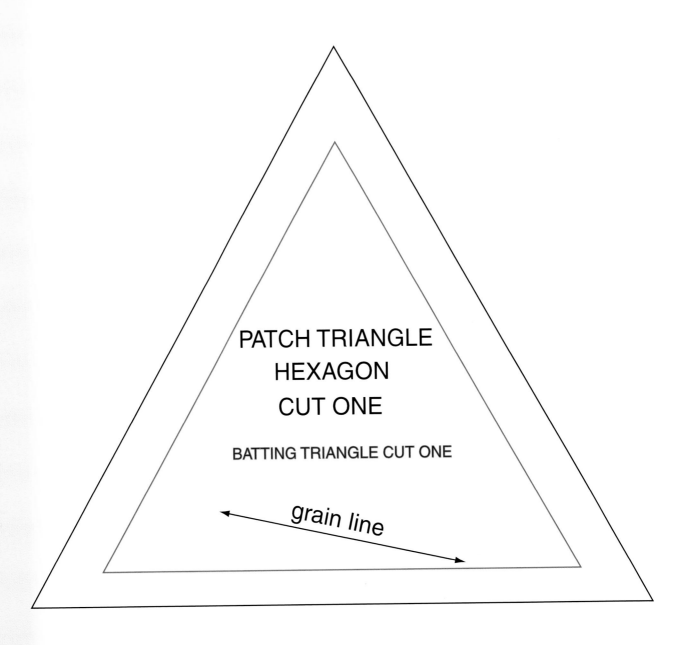

PATCH TRIANGLE
HEXAGON
CUT ONE

BATTING TRIANGLE CUT ONE

grain line

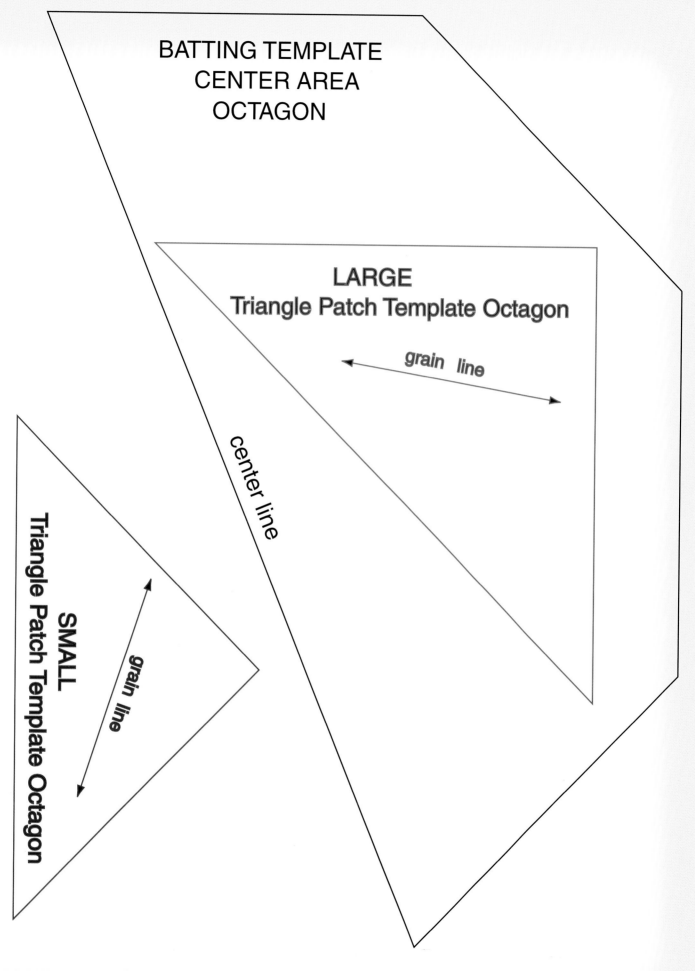

BATTING TEMPLATE
CENTER AREA
OCTAGON

LARGE
Triangle Patch Template Octagon

grain line

center line

SMALL
Triangle Patch Template Octagon

grain line

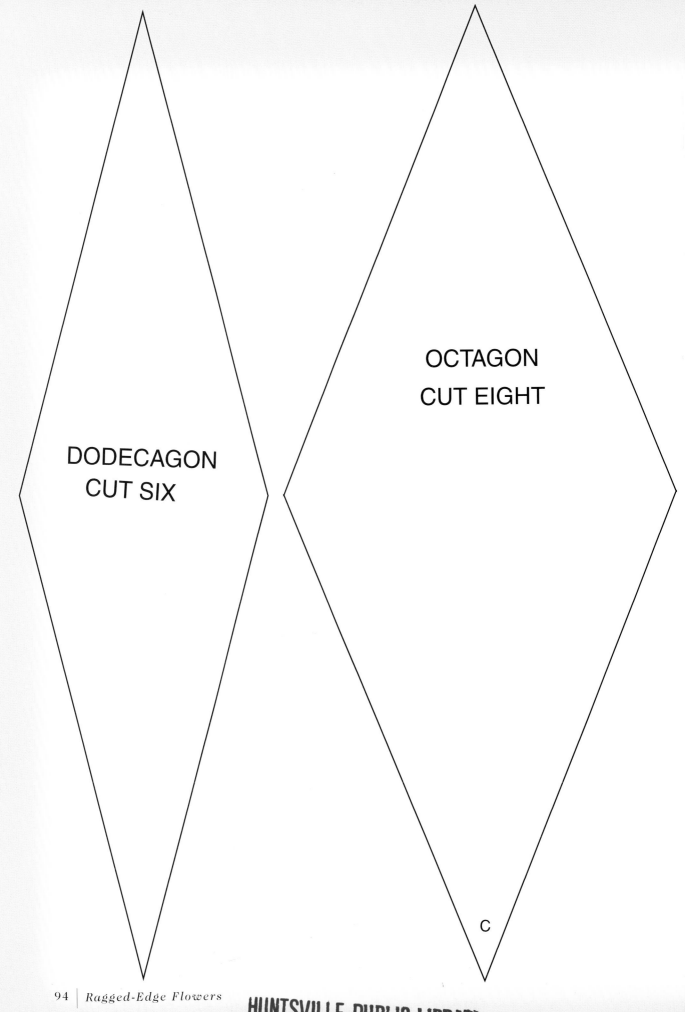

DODECAGON
CUT SIX

OCTAGON
CUT EIGHT

C

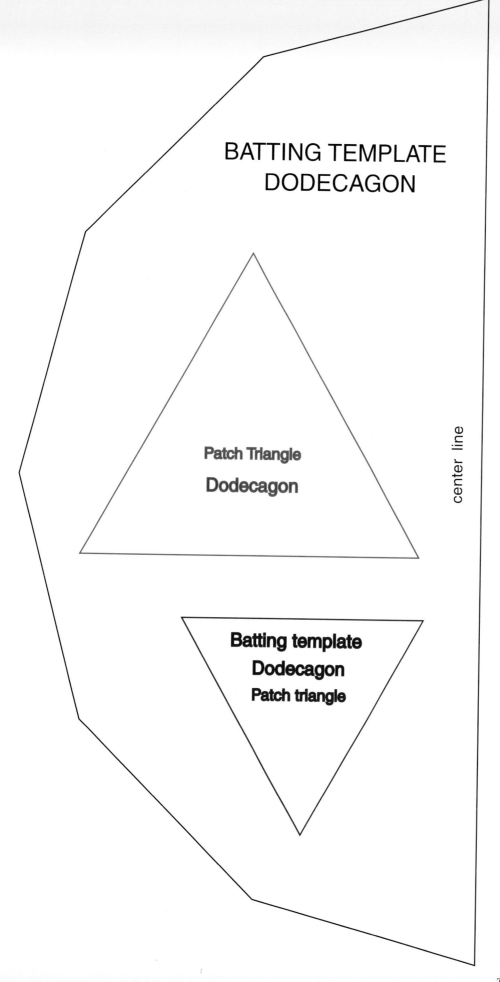

BATTING TEMPLATE
DODECAGON

Patch Triangle

Dodecagon

center line

Batting template

Dodecagon

Patch triangle

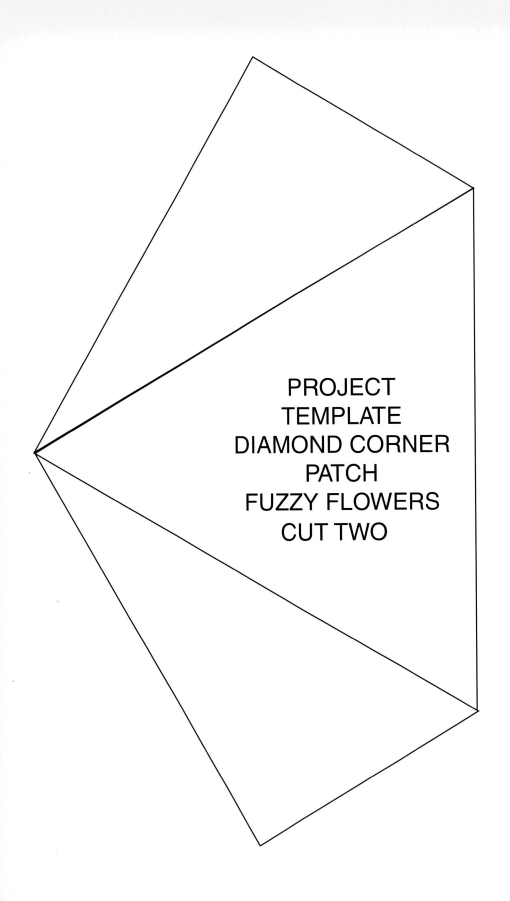

PROJECT
TEMPLATE
DIAMOND CORNER
PATCH
FUZZY FLOWERS
CUT TWO